Can Humanity Change?

Books by J. Krishnamurti

Can
Humanity
Change?

*J. Krishnamurti
in Dialogue with
Buddhists*

EDITED BY DAVID SKITT

Shambhala
Boston & London
2003

Shambhala Publications, Inc.
Horticultural Hall
300 Massachusetts Avenue
Boston, Massachusetts 02115
www.shambhala.com

Pages 223–224 constitute a continuation of this copyright page.

The editor wishes to thank Professor Mahinda Palihawadana,
Mr. Panduka Mendis, and Mr. Daya Ratnasekara for help with the Pali
and Sanskrit terms and with the checking of transcripts.

9 8 7 6 5 4 3 2

Printed in the United States of America

♾ This edition is printed on acid-free paper that meets the
American National Standards Institute Z39.48 Standard.
Distributed in the United States by Random House, Inc.,
and in Canada by Random House of Canada Ltd

Library of Congress Cataloging-in-Publication Data

Can humanity change?: J. Krishnamurti in dialogue with Buddhists/
edited by David Skitt.
p. cm.
ISBN-13 978-1-59030-072-5
ISBN-10 1-59030-072-6
1. Krishnamurti, J. (Jiddu), 1895—Interviews. 2.
Buddhists—Interviews 3. Self. 4. Conduct of life. I. Skitt, David.
B5134.K754C36 2003
181'.4—dc21
2003005253

Contents

Introduction

Is what is happening in the world pointing to the need for a fundamental change in human consciousness, and is such a change possible? This is an issue at the heart of both Krishnamurti's and the Buddha's teaching, and in 1978 and 1979 the eminent Buddhist scholar Walpola Rahula came to Brockwood Park in England to put questions that had occurred to him from his reading of Krishnamurti's books. The future Chancellor of the Sri Lankan University of Buddhist and Pali Studies, Walpola Rahula was an acknowledged authority on both the Theravada and the Mahayana schools of Buddhism. He had lectured at universities around the world, and was the author of the article on the Buddha in the *Encyclopedia Britannica*. He had also written a widely known introduction to Buddhism, translated into many languages, called *What the Buddha Taught*. He was accompanied by Irmgard Schloegl, a well-known teacher of Zen Buddhism and for some years the librarian of the Buddhist Society of London.

Nearly all the conversations, in which the physicist David Bohm and the scientist and author Phiroz Mehta also participated, start with Dr. Rahula raising an issue of crucial importance for any radical change in the way we usually see ourselves, others, life, and death. The nature of personal identity, whether there is a relative truth and an ultimate truth, and the distinction between insight and intellectual understanding are all topics on which he argues that the Buddha and Krishnamurti have said substantially the same things. He also explains to Krishnamurti that in his view the original teaching of the Buddha has over the centuries been in many ways misunderstood and misinterpreted, particularly with regard to the nature of meditation and the form of meditation known as *satipatthana*, or "mindfulness."

On each occasion, however, instead of discussing whether Dr. Rahula's argument is right or wrong, Krishnamurti moves the debate into quite a different direction. Why, he asks, compare? What is the value of such comparison? Why bring the Buddha into the discussion between the two of them? Courteously, and with a lightness of tone, Krishnamurti challenges Walpola Rahula to say whether he is taking part in the conversation as a Buddhist or as a human being, whether he considers that humanity is in any sense progressing psychologically, what he understands by the word "love."

Dr. Rahula continues, however, in most of these conversations to draw parallels between what the Buddha has said and what Krishnamurti is saying, so that a reader interested in that inquiry will find much of interest. But at another level there is something quite different going on. Time and time again after describing, say, the role of thought in creating the self, Krishnamurti will ask Dr. Rahula and the other participants: Do you *see* that? The word *see* is rightly emphasized, because the seeing in question is clearly meant to be seeing with such depth and clarity that consciousness and simultaneously action are radically transformed. It is also notable that Krishnamurti unfolds his argument by a series of questions, some of which he wants his listeners to allow to sink in rather than to answer—a distinction they do not always find it easy to make.

This moves the debate into an area which all of us are familiar with, to some extent at least—understanding verbally, rather than understanding so deeply that we change our behavior. There must be few of us who have not looked at something we have done and said, "I can see why I did that, and I shouldn't have done it," yet do exactly the same thing a short time later. "I shouldn't have taken that criticism personally." "I shouldn't have lost patience." "I shouldn't have said that, it really doesn't help." In all these cases one may be able to express with great clarity the reasons why one did what one did and should not do it, and then find oneself doing precisely that again. In other words, our understanding was purely verbal or intellectual, lacking what one might call a radical insight, and definitely not of the kind that we refer to when we say, "Then I *really* understood."

So what brings about a fundamental change in a human being? And one that brings about an endless, unfolding awareness? This is a question that runs like a silken thread throughout these conversations. Repeatedly Walpola Rahula says all the right words, and Krishnamurti does not deny that his Buddhist questioner may well see the truth to which these words refer. But Krishnamurti urges him to go further and to explain how such seeing comes about, and to discuss the nature and quality of the mind that has such clarity. This is really the kernel of the encounter.

Most of this book consists of these five conversations. Since, however, they are concerned with barriers to deep shifts of perception, the book also contains a final section of questions in which people who find they have not changed after listening to Krishnamurti ask him to account for this. The various and sometimes vigorous answers he gives may be of as much interest to Buddhists as to students of Krishnamurti, and to readers in neither of these two groups.

What is one to make of this encounter? This seems like a question whose very nature demands that the answer, if there is one, be left solely to the reader.

DAVID SKITT

Part One

Are You Not Saying
What the Buddha Said?

*First Conversation with the Buddhist Scholars
Walpola Rahula and Irmgard Schloegl, and with
Professor David Bohm and Others*

WALPOLA RAHULA: I have been following your teaching—if I may use that word—from my younger days. I have read most of your books with great, with deep interest, and I have wanted to have this discussion with you for a long time.

To someone who knows the Buddha's teaching fairly well, your teaching is quite familiar, not something new to him. What the Buddha taught twenty-five hundred years ago you teach today in a new idiom, a new style, a new garb. When I read your books I often write in the margin, comparing what you say with the Buddha; sometimes I even quote the chapter and verse of the text—not only Buddha's original teaching, but also the ideas of the later Buddhist philosophers, those too you put in practically the same way. I was surprised how well and beautifully you expressed them.

So to begin with, I want to mention briefly a few points that are common to Buddha's teaching and to yours. For instance, Buddha did not accept the notion of a creator God who rules this world and rewards and punishes people for their actions. Nor do you, I believe. Buddha did not accept the old Vedic, Brahmanic idea of an eternal, permanent everlasting, unchanging soul or atman—Buddha denied this. Nor do you, I think, accept that notion.

Buddha begins his teaching from the premise that human life is a predicament, suffering, conflict, sorrow. And your books always emphasize that. Also, Buddha says that what causes this conflict, this suffering, is the selfishness created by the wrong idea of self, my self, my atman. I think you say that too.

Buddha says that when one is free from desire, from attachment, from the self, one is free from suffering and conflict. And you said somewhere, I remember, that freedom means freedom from all attachment. That is exactly what Buddha taught—from *all* attachment. There is no discrimination between attachment that is good and attachment that is bad—of course there is in ordinary practical life, but ultimately there is no such division.

Then there is the seeing of truth, the realization of truth, that is, to see things as they are; as the Buddha says, in Buddhist terminology, *yatha bhutam*. When you do that, you see reality, you see truth and are free from conflict. I think you have said this very often—in, for example, the book *Truth and Actuality*. This is quite well known in Buddhist thought as *samvriti-satya* and *paramartha-satya*: *samvriti-satya* is the conventional truth, and *paramartha-satya* is the absolute or ultimate truth. And you cannot see the ultimate or absolute truth without seeing the conventional or relative truth. That is the Buddhist attitude. And I think you say the same thing.

On the more popular level, but very importantly, you always say that you must not depend on authority—anybody's authority, anybody's teaching. You must realize it yourself, see it for yourself.

This is a very well known teaching in Buddhism. Buddha told the Kalamas, Don't accept anything just because it is said by religion or scripture, or by a teacher or guru, only accept it if you see for yourself that it is right; if you see it is wrong or bad, then reject it.

In a very interesting discussion that you had with Swami Venkatesananda, he asked about the importance of gurus, and your answer was always: What can a guru do? It is up to you to do it, a guru can't save you. This is exactly the Buddhist attitude—that you should not accept authority. After reading the whole of this discussion in your book *The Awakening of Intelligence*, I wrote that Buddha has said these things too, and summarized them in two lines in the *Dhammapada: tumhehi kiccam atappam/ akkhataro tathagata*—you must make the effort, the Buddhas only teach. This is in the *Dhammapada*, which you read long ago when you were young.

Another very important thing is your emphasis on awareness or mindfulness. This is something that, as explained in the *Satipatthana-sutta*, is extremely important in Buddha's teaching, to be aware, to be mindful. I myself was surprised when I read in the *Mahaparinibbana-sutta*, a discourse about the last month of his life, that wherever he stopped and talked to his disciples he always said: Be aware, cultivate awareness, mindfulness. It is called *satipatthana*, the presence of awareness or mindfulness. This is also a very strong point in your teaching, which I very much appreciate and follow.

Then another interesting thing is your constant emphasis on impermanence. This is one of the fundamental things in Buddha's teaching: everything is impermanent, and there is nothing that is permanent. And in the book *Freedom from the Known*, you have said that to discover nothing is permanent is of tremendous importance; for only then is the mind free. That is in complete accordance with the Four Noble Truths of the Buddha.

There is another lesser but interesting point showing how your teaching and the Buddha's go together. I think in *Freedom from the Known*, you say that control and outward discipline are not the way, nor has an undisciplined life any value. When I read this, I wrote in the margin: A Brahmin asked the Buddha: How did you attain these spiritual heights, by what precepts, what discipline, what knowledge? Buddha answered: Not by knowledge, not by discipline, not by precepts, nor without them. That is the important thing—not with these things, but not without them either. It is exactly what you say: you condemn slavery to discipline, but without discipline life has no value. That is exactly how it is in Zen Buddhism—there is no Zen Buddhism, Zen is Buddhism. In Zen, slavery to discipline is seen as attachment, and that is very much condemned, but there is no Buddhist sect in the world where discipline is so much emphasized.

We have many other things to talk about, but to begin with I want to say that there is fundamental agreement on these things, and there is no conflict between you and the Buddha. Of course you are not a Buddhist, as you say.

KRISHNAMURTI: No, sir.

WR: And I myself don't know what I am, it does not matter. But there is hardly any difference between your teaching and the Buddha's; it is just that you say the same thing in a way that is fascinating for today's human beings, and for those of tomorrow. And now I would like to know what you think about all this.

K: May I ask, sir, with due respect, why you compare?

WR: This is because when I read your books as a Buddhist scholar, as one who has studied Buddhist texts, I always see that it is the same thing.

K: Yes, sir, but if I may ask, what is the necessity of comparing?

WR: There is no necessity at all.

K: If you were not a scholar of Buddhism and all the sutras and sayings of the Buddha, if you had not gone very deeply into Buddhism, how would it strike you on reading these books, without the background of all that?

WR: That I can't tell you, because I was never without that background. One is conditioned, it is a conditioning. We are all conditioned. Therefore I cannot answer that question because I don't know what the position would be.

K: So if I may point out, I hope you don't mind . . .

WR: No, not at all.

K: Does knowledge condition human beings—knowledge of scriptures, knowledge of what the saints have said and so on, the whole gamut of so-called sacred books, does that help humanity at all?

WR: Scriptures and all our knowledge condition human beings, there is no doubt about that. But I should say that knowledge is not absolutely unnecessary. Buddha has pointed out very clearly that if you want to cross the river and there is no bridge, you build a boat and cross with its help. But if, on the other shore, you think, Oh, this boat has been very useful, very helpful to me, I can't leave it here, I will carry it on my shoulders, that is a wrong action. What you should say is: Of course this boat was very helpful to me, but I have crossed the river, it is no more use to me, so I'll leave it here for somebody else. That is the attitude toward knowledge and learning. Buddha says that even the teachings, not only that, even the virtues, the so-called moral virtues, are also like the boat and have a relative and conditioned value.

K: I am not doubting what you are saying, sir, but I would like to question whether knowledge has the quality of liberating the mind.

WR: I don't think knowledge can liberate.

K: Knowledge can't, but the quality, the strength, the sense of capacity, the sense of value that you derive from knowledge, the feeling that you know, the weight of knowledge—doesn't that strengthen the self?

WR: Certainly.

K: Does knowledge actually condition the human being? Let's put it that way. The word "knowledge" all of us surely take to mean accumulation of information, of experience, of various facts, theories and principles, the past and present, all that bundle we call knowledge. Does, then, the past help? Because knowledge *is* the past.

WR: All that past, all that knowledge, disappears the moment you see the truth.

K: But can a mind that is burdened with knowledge see truth?

WR: Of course, if the mind is burdened, crowded, and covered with knowledge . . .

K: It is, generally it is. Most minds are filled and crippled with knowledge. I am using the word "crippled" in the sense of weighed down. Can such a mind perceive what is truth? Or must it be free from knowledge?

WR: To see the truth the mind must be free from all knowledge.

K: Yes, so why should one accumulate knowledge and then abandon it, and then seek truth? You follow what I am saying?

WR: Well, I think that in our ordinary life, most of the things which we have learned are useful at the beginning. For instance, as schoolchildren we can't write without ruled paper, but today I can write without it.

K: Wait a minute, sir, I agree. When you are at school or university we need lines to write on and all the rest of it, but does not the beginning, which might condition the future as we grow up, matter enormously? You understand what I am saying? I don't know if I am making myself clear. Does freedom lie at the end or at the beginning?

WR: Freedom has no beginning, no end.

K: Would you say that freedom is limited by knowledge?

WR: Freedom is not limited by knowledge; perhaps knowledge that is acquired and wrongly applied may obstruct freedom.

K: No, there is no wrong or right accumulation of knowledge. I may do certain ugly things and repent, or carry on with those ugly things, which again is part of my knowledge. But I am asking if knowledge leads to freedom. As you say, discipline is necessary at the beginning. And as you grow older, mature, acquire capacities and so on, does that discipline not condition the mind so that it can never abandon discipline in the usual sense of that word?

WR: Yes, I understand. You agree that discipline at the beginning, at a certain level, is necessary.

K: I am questioning that, sir. When I say questioning it, I don't mean I doubt it or am saying it is not necessary, but I am questioning it in order to inquire.

WR: I should say at a certain level it is necessary, but then if you can never abandon it . . . I am talking from the Buddhist point of view. There are two terms in Buddhism with regard to the Way, *shaikshya* and *ashaikshya: shaikshya* refers to people who are on the Way but have not yet arrived, for whom there are disciplines, precepts, and all those things that are good and bad, right and wrong. And an arhat who has realized the truth is called *ashaikshya* and has no discipline, because he is beyond that.

K: Yes, I understand this.

WR: But that is a fact in life.

K: I am questioning that, sir.

WR: I have no doubt about it in my mind.

K: Then we have stopped inquiring.

WR: No, it is not so.

K: I mean we are talking about knowledge: knowledge being

useful or necessary, as a boat to cross the river. I want to inquire into that fact or that simile to see whether it is the truth, whether it has the quality of truth—let us put it that way for the moment.

WR: You mean the simile or the teaching?

K: The whole of that. Which means, sir—just a minute—which means accepting evolution.

WR: Yes, accepting it.

K: Evolution, so gradually, step by step, advancing, and ultimately reaching. First I discipline, control, use effort, and as I get more capacity, more energy, more strength, I abandon that and move on.

WR: There is no plan like that, there is no plan.

K: No, I am not saying there is a plan. I am asking, or inquiring, whether there is such a movement, such progress at all.

WR: What do you think?

K: What do I think? No.

IRMGARD SCHLOEGL: I very much agree with you, I can't believe that there is.

WR: Yes, all right, there is no progress like that.

K: We must go into this very carefully, because the whole religious tradition, Buddhist, Hindu, and Christian, all the religious and nonreligious attitudes are caught up in time, in evolution—I will be better, I will be good, I will eventually blossom in goodness. Right? I am saying that there is a root of untruth in this. Sorry to put it that way.

IS: I entirely agree with that, for the very good reason that as far as we know, ever since human beings have existed, we have always known that we should be good. If it were possible to progress by something like this we would not be the human beings that we are today. We would all have progressed sufficiently.

K: Have we progressed at all?

IS: Precisely, we have not progressed—very little, if at all.

K: We may have progressed technologically, scientifically, hygienically, and all the rest of it, but psychologically, inwardly we have not—we are what we were ten thousand or more years ago.

IS: So the fact that we know we should do good, and have evolved so many systems of how to do it, has not managed to help us to become good. As I see it, there is a specific obstacle in all of us, and it is the working through this obstacle—because most of us want in our hearts to be good, but most of us do not bring it about—that seems to me at stake.

K: We have accepted evolution. Biologically there is evolution. We have transferred that biological fact into psychological existence, thinking that we will evolve psychologically.

WR: No, I don't think that is the attitude.

K: But that is what it means when you say "gradually."

WR: No, I don't say "gradually." I don't say that. The realization of truth, attainment of truth, or seeing the truth, is without a plan, is without a scheme.

K: It is out of time.

WR: Out of time, exactly.

K: Which is quite different from saying that my mind—which has evolved through centuries, for millennia, which is conditioned by time, which is evolution, which is the acquiring of more and more knowledge—will reveal the extraordinary truth.

WR: It is not that knowledge will reveal truth.

K: Therefore why should I accumulate knowledge?

WR: How can you avoid it?

K: Avoid it psychologically, not technologically.

WR: Even psychologically, how can you do that?

K: Ah, that's a different matter.

WR: Yes, how can you do that? Because you are conditioned.

K: Wait a minute, sir. Let's go into it a little more. Biologically, physically, from childhood up to a certain age, adolescence, maturity and so on, we evolve, that is a fact. A little oak tree grows into a gigantic oak tree, that is a fact. Now, is it a fact, or have we simply assumed it is, that we must grow psychologically? Which means, psychologically, that eventually I will achieve truth, or truth will take place if I prepare the ground.

WR: No, that is a wrong conclusion, that is a wrong point of view, the realization of truth is a revolution, not evolution.

K: Therefore, can the mind be free psychologically of the idea of progress?

WR: It can be.

K: No, not "can be," it must be.

WR: That is what I have said—revolution is not evolution, not a gradual process.

K: So psychologically, can there be a revolution?

WR: Yes, certainly.

K: Which means what? No time.

WR: There is no time in it.

K: But all the religions, all the scriptures, whether it is Islam or whatever, have maintained you must go through certain systems.

WR: But not Buddhism.

K: Wait a minute. I wouldn't even say Buddhism, I don't know, I haven't read about it, except when I was a boy, but that has gone out of my mind. When you say that you must have discipline first and then eventually let go of that discipline . . .

WR: No, I don't say that. I don't postulate it like that, and neither did the Buddha.

K: Then, please, I may be mistaken.

WR: The question I have to ask you is: How does the realization of truth come about?

K: Ah, that's quite a different matter.

WR: What I am saying is that we are conditioned. Nobody can avoid that, however much they try. The revolution is to see that you are conditioned. The moment you see that, it has no time, it is an entire revolution, and that is the truth.

K: Suppose one is conditioned in the pattern of evolution—I have been, I am, I shall be. That is evolution, isn't it? My action was ugly yesterday, but today I am learning about that ugliness and freeing myself and tomorrow I will be free of it. That is our whole attitude, the psychological structure of our being. This is an everyday fact.

WR: Do we see that? Understanding may be intellectual, merely verbal.

K: No, I am not talking either intellectually or verbally, I mean that is a fact. I will try to be good.

WR: There is no question of trying to be good.

K: No, sir, not according to the Buddha, not according to scripture, but the average human being in everyday life says, "I am not as good as I should be, but—give me a couple of weeks or years, and eventually I will be awfully good."

WR: Certainly that is the attitude that practically everybody has.

K: Practically everybody. Now wait a minute. That is our conditioning—the Christian, the Buddhist, the whole world is conditioned by this idea, which may have come from biological progress and moved into the psychological field.

WR: Yes, that's a good way of putting it.

K: Now, how is a man or woman, a human being, to break this pattern without bringing in time? You understand my question?

WR: Yes, it is only by seeing.

K: No, I can't see if I am caught in this blasted ugliness of progress. You say it is only by seeing, and I say I can't see.

WR: Then you can't.

K: No, but I want to inquire into it, sir. That is, why have we given "progress," in quotes, such psychological importance?

IS: I am not a scholar but a practitioner. For me personally as a Westerner, as a one-time scientist, I have found the most satisfactory answer in the Buddhist teaching that I blind myself, I am my own obstacle. As long as I, with all my bundle of conditioning, am here, I cannot see and act. There seems to be a possibility . . .

K: That doesn't help me. You are saying that you have learned that.

IS: I have learned it, but I have done so in the same way as one learns to play the piano, rather than in the way of studying a subject.

K: Again, playing the piano, which means practice. So what are we talking about at the end of all this?

GIDDU NARAYAN: There seems to be a difficulty here. Knowledge has a certain fascination, a certain power, one accumulates knowledge, whether it is Buddhist or scientific, and it gives you a peculiar sense of freedom, though it is not freedom—it is more in the realm of conventional freedom. And after years of study one finds it very difficult to get out of this, because for twenty or so years you arrive at this point and value it, but it hasn't got the quality of what you might call truth. The difficulty with all practice seems to be that when you practice you achieve something; and the achievement is of the conventional-reality type, it has got a certain power, a certain fascination, a certain capacity, maybe a certain clarity.

WR: Because of that you get attached to it.

GN: Yes, and to break away from it is much more difficult than for a beginner; a beginner who has not got these things may see something more directly than a man who has a great deal of acquired wisdom.

WR: That depends on the individual; you can't generalize.

K: If I may point out, one can generalize as a principle. But let us come back to where we were. We are all caught in this idea of progress, of attainment, right?

WR: We had just come to an agreement on that point, that humanity accepts the fact that progress is a gradual evolution. As you said, they accept it as true biologically and can prove it there, so they apply the same theory to the psychological area. We agreed that that is the human position.

K: Is that position the truth? I have accepted that there is progress in the sense of biological evolution and have then gradually transferred that to psychological existence. Now, is that the truth?

WR: Now I see what you are questioning. I don't think it is the truth.

K: Therefore I abandon the whole idea of discipline.

WR: I should have said there is no question of abandoning it. If you abandon it consciously . . .

K: No, sir, just a minute. I see what human beings have done, which is to move from the biological to the psychological, and there they have invented this idea that eventually you will come

15

to the godhead or enlightenment, reach Brahman or whatever, nirvana or paradise, or hell. If you see the falseness of that, actually not theoretically, then it is finished.

WR: Absolutely, that is what I have been saying all the time.

K: Why should I then acquire knowledge of scriptures, of this or that, psychologically?

WR: There is no reason.

K: Then why do I read the Buddha?

WR: As I have said, we are all conditioned.

DAVID BOHM: Could I ask a question: Do you accept that we are all conditioned?

K: Dr. Bohm asks: Do we all accept that we are conditioned?

WR: I don't know whether you accept it or not, I accept it. To be in time is to be conditioned.

DB: Well, what I mean to say is this: I think that Krishnaji has said, at least in some of our discussions, that he was not deeply conditioned in the beginning, and therefore had a certain insight that would not be common. Is that fair?

K: Please, don't refer to me—I may be a biological freak, so leave me out of it. What we are trying to discuss, sir, is this: Can we admit the truth that psychologically there is no movement forward—the truth of it, not the idea of it? You understand?

WR: I understand.

K: The truth of it, not "I accept the idea of it," the idea is not the truth. So do we as human beings see the truth or falseness of what we have done?

WR: You mean, human beings generally?

K: The whole world.

WR: No, they don't see it.

K: Therefore when you tell them, Get more knowledge, read this, read that, scriptures, what the Buddha said, what Christ said, if he existed at all, and so on, they are full of this accumulative instinct that will help them to jump or propel themselves into heaven.

DB: When we say we are all conditioned, how do we know that we are all conditioned? That is really what I wanted to say.

K: Yes, his point is, sir, are all human beings conditioned?

WR: That is a very complicated question. As far as our society is concerned, all are conditioned. There can't be anybody who is not conditioned, because he is within time. But what we are talking about is the realization of truth, which has no time, which is unconditioned.

DB: What I wanted to emphasize is that if we say we are all conditioned, there could be two ways of responding to that. One way could be to accumulate knowledge about our conditioning, to say we observe the common human experience, we can look at people and see that they are generally conditioned. The other way would be to say, Do we see in a more direct way that we are all conditioned? That's what I was trying to get at.

WR: Of course, I should say that there are people who see that.

K: But does that help in this matter? I mean there may or there may not be.

DB: The only point I am trying to make is that if we say that we are all conditioned, then I think there is nothing else to do but some kind of disciplined or gradual approach. That is, you begin with your conditioning.

K: Not necessarily. I don't see that.

DB: Well, let's try to pursue this. That's the way I take the implication of Dr. Rahula's question that if we all begin conditioned . . .

K: Which we are.

DB: Then what can we do for the next step?

WR: There is nothing called "the next step."

DB: How can we be free of the conditioning as we do whatever we do?

WR: The freedom from conditioning is to see.

DB: Well, the same question: How do we see?

WR: Of course many people have tried various ways.

K: No, there are not various ways. The moment you say "a way," you have already conditioned it.

WR: That is what I say. And you are also conditioning by your talks, they are also conditioning. Trying to uncondition the mind is also conditioning it.

K: No, I question that statement, whether what K is talking about conditions the mind—the mind being the brain, thoughts, feelings, the whole human psychological existence. I doubt it, I question it. If I may suggest, we are going off from the central issue.

WR: The question is how to see—is that it?

K: No, sir, no. Not "how," there is no "how." First let us see this simple fact: Do I, as a human being, see that I am representative of all humanity—I am a human being, and therefore I represent all humanity. Right?

IS: In an individual way.

K: No, as a human being, I represent you, the whole world, because I suffer, I go through agony and so on, so does every human being. So do I, as a human being, see the false step human beings have taken by moving from the biological to the psychological with the same mentality? There, biologically, there is progress, from the little to the big and so on, from the wheel to the jet. As a human being, do I see the mischief that human beings have created by moving from there to this? Do I see it, as I see this table? Or do I say, "Yes, I accept the theory of it, the idea of it," and then we are lost. And the theory, the idea, is therefore knowledge.

IS: If I see it as I see this table, then it is no longer a theory.

K: It is then a fact. But the moment you move away from the fact, it becomes idea, knowledge, and the pursuit of that. You move further away from the fact. I don't know if I am making myself clear.

WR: Yes, I guess that is so.

K: What is so? Human beings moving away?

WR: Human beings are caught in this.

K: Yes, it is a fact, isn't it, that there is biological progress, from a little tree to a gigantic tree, from baby to boyhood and to adolescence. Now have we moved with that mentality, with that idea, with that fact, into the psychological field, and assumed as a fact that we progress there, which is a false movement? I wonder if I am making myself clear.

DB: Are you saying that this is part of the conditioning?

K: No, leave the conditioning aside for the moment. I don't want to enter into that. But why have we applied the fact of biological growth to the psychological field? It is a fact that we have, but why have we done this?

IS: I want to become something.

K: Which is, you want satisfaction, safety, certainty, a sense of achievement.

IS: And it is in the wanting.

K: So why doesn't a human being see what he has done—actually, not theoretically?

IS: An ordinary human being.

K: You, I, X,Y.

IS: I do not like to see it, I fear it.

K: Therefore you are living in an illusion.

IS: Naturally.

K: Why?

IS: I want to be something that I fear at the same time not to see. This is where the "why" is.

K: No, madam, when you see what you have done, there is no fear.

IS: But the fact is that I usually do not see it.

K: Why don't you see it?

IS: I suspect because of fear. I don't know why.

K: You are entering into quite a different field when you talk of fear. I would just like to inquire why human beings have done this, played this game for millennia. Why this living in this false structure, and then people come along and say be unselfish, be this and all the rest of it—why?

IS: All of us have a very strong irrational side in us.

K: I am questioning all this, because we are living not with facts but with ideas and knowledge.

WR: Certainly.

K: The fact is that biologically there is evolution, and psychologically there is not. And so we give importance to knowledge, ideas, theories, philosophy, and all the rest of it.

WR: You don't see at all that there can be a certain development, an evolution, even psychologically?

K: No.

WR: But take a man with a bad criminal record who lies, steals, and so on—you can explain to him certain very fundamental, elementary things, and he changes, in the conventional sense, into a better man, no longer stealing, no longer telling lies or wanting to kill others.

K: A terrorist, for example.

WR: A man like that can change.

K: Are you saying, sir, a man who is evil, "evil" in quotes, like the terrorists around the world, what is their future? Are you asking that?

WR: Don't you agree that you can explain to a criminal like that the wrongness of his behavior? Because he understands what you have said, either because of his own thinking or because of your personal influence or whatever, he transforms himself, he changes.

K: I am not sure, sir, whether you can talk to a criminal, in the orthodox sense of that word, at all.

WR: That I don't know.

K: You can pacify him, you know, give him a reward and this and that, but an actual criminally minded man, will he ever listen to any sanity? The terrorist—will he listen to you, to your sanity? Of course not.

WR: That you can't say. I don't know, I am not at all positive about it. But until I have more proof, I can't say that.

K: I have no proof either, but you can see what is happening.

WR: What is happening is that there are terrorists, and we don't know whether any of them have transformed themselves into good men. We have no proof.

K: You see that is my whole point—the bad man evolving into the good man.

21

WR: In the popular and the conventional sense, that certainly happens, one can't deny that.

K: Yes, we know that, we have dozens of examples.

WR: Don't we accept that at all?

K: No, wait a minute, sir. A bad man who tells lies, is cruel and so on, probably one day he realizes it is an ugly business and says, "I'll change and become good," but that is not goodness. Goodness is not born out of badness.

WR: Certainly not.

K: Therefore the "bad man," in quotes, can never become the good man, non-quotes. Goodness is not the opposite of the bad.

WR: At that level it is.

K: At any level.

WR: I don't agree.

GN: We might put it this way. At the conventional level the bad man becomes the good man. I think we would call that "psychological progress." That's something we do, the human mind does.

K: Of course, you are wearing yellow and I am wearing brown, we have the opposites of night and day, man and woman, and so on. But is there an opposite of fear? Is there an opposite of goodness? Is love the opposite of hate? The opposite, which means duality.

WR: I would say that we are talking in dualistic terms.

K: All language is dualistic.

WR: You can't talk, I can't talk, without a dualistic approach.

K: Yes, for comparing. But I am not talking of that.

WR: At the present moment you are speaking about the absolute, the ultimate. When we talk of good and bad we are talking dualistically.

K: No, that's why I want to move away.

WR: You can't talk about the absolute in terms of good or bad. There is nothing called absolute good or bad.

K: No. Is courage the opposite of fear? That is, if fear is nonexistent, is it courage? Or is it something totally different?

IS: It is something totally different.

K: Therefore it is not the opposite. Goodness is never the opposite of bad. So what are we talking about when we say, "I will move, change, from my conditioning, which is bad, to freedom from my conditioning, which is good"? Therefore freedom is the opposite of my conditioning. Therefore it is not freedom at all. That freedom is born out of my conditioning because I am caught in this prison and I want to be free. It is a reaction to the prison, which is not freedom.

WR: I don't quite follow.

K: Sir, could we consider for a minute: Is love the opposite of hate?

WR: The only thing you can say is, where there is love there is no hate.

K: No, I am asking a different question. I am asking: Is hate the opposite of affection, love? If it is, then in that affection, in that love, there is hate, because it is born out of hate, out of the opposite. All opposites are born out of their own opposites. No?

WR: I don't know. That is what you say.

· K: But it is a fact, sir. Look, I am afraid, and I cultivate courage. You know, in order to put away fear I take a drink, or whatever, all the rest of it, to get rid of fear. And at the end of it I say that I am very courageous. All the war heroes and the rest of them are given medals for this. Because they are frightened, they say, "we must go and kill" or do something or other, and they become very courageous, heroes.

WR: That is not courage.

K: I am saying anything born out of its opposite contains its own opposite.

WR: How?

K: Sir, if someone hates you and then says, "I must love," that love is born out of hate. Because he knows what hate is, and he says, "I must not be this, but I must be that." So that is the opposite of this. Therefore that opposite contains this.

WR: I don't know whether it is the opposite.

K: That is how we live, sir. This is what we do. I am sexual, I must not be sexual. I take a vow of celibacy—not "I," people take a vow of celibacy, which is the opposite. So they are always caught in this corridor of opposites. And I question the whole corridor. I don't think it exists; we have invented it, but actually it doesn't exist. I mean, please, this is just an explanation; don't accept anything, sir.

IS: Personally, I regard, as a working hypothesis, this channel of opposites as a humanizing factor, and we are caught in it.

K: Oh no, that is not a humanizing factor. That is like saying, "I have been a tribal entity, now I have become a nation, and then ultimately I will become international." It is still tribalism going on.

DB: I think both of you are saying that we do in some sense make progress in that we are not as barbaric as we were before.

IS: That is what I mean by the humanizing factor.

K: I question whether it is humanizing.

WR: I don't like to go to extremes.

K: These are not extremes, these are just facts. Facts are not extremes.

DB: Are you saying that this is not genuine progress? In the past, people were far more barbaric than they generally are today, and would you say that this really doesn't mean very much?

K: We are still barbarous.

DB: Yes, we are, but some people say we are not as barbaric as we were.

K: Not *as*.

DB: Let's see if we can get this straight. Now, would you say that this is not important, that this is not significant?

K: No, when I say I am better than I was, it has no meaning.

DB: I think we should clarify that.

WR: In the relative, dualistic sense I don't accept that, I can't see that. But in the absolute, ultimate sense there is nothing like that.

K: No, not ultimately— I won't even accept that word, "ultimately." I see how the opposite is born in everyday life, not ultimately. I am greedy, that is a fact. I try to become non-greedy, which is non-fact, but if I remain with the fact that I am greedy, then I can do something about it actually now. Therefore there is no opposite. Sir, take violence and nonviolence. Nonviolence is the opposite of violence, an ideal. So nonviolence is non-fact. Violence is the only fact. So I can then deal with facts, not with non-facts.

WR: So what is your point?

K: My point is that there is no duality even in daily life. It is the invention of all the philosophers, intellectuals, utopians, idealists who say there is the opposite, work for that. The fact is I am

25

violent, that is all, let me deal with that. And to deal with it, don't invent nonviolence.

IS: The question now is: How am I going to deal with it, having accepted the fact that I am violent?

K: Not accepted, it's a fact.

IS: Having seen it.

K: Then we can proceed, I'll show you. But first I must see what I am doing now. I am avoiding the fact and running away to non-fact. That is what is happening all over the world. So don't run, but remain with the fact. Can you do it?

IS: Well, the question is, can one do it? One can, but one often does not like doing it.

K: Of course you can do it. It's like seeing something dangerous and saying, "It's dangerous, so I won't go near it." Running away from the fact is dangerous. So that's finished, you don't run away. That doesn't mean you train, that you practice not to run, you don't run. I think the gurus, the philosophers, have invented the running. Sorry.

WR: There is no running away, that is entirely different, it is a wrong way of putting it.

K: No, sir.

WR: You can't run away.

K: No, I am saying, don't run, then you see, don't run, then you see. But we say, "I can't see because I am caught in that."

WR: I quite see that, I see your point very well.

K: So there is no duality.

WR: Where?

K: Now, in daily life, not ultimately.

WR: What is duality?

K: Duality is the opposite, violence and nonviolence. You know, the whole of India has been practicing nonviolence, which is nonsense. There is only violence, let me deal with that. Let human beings deal with violence, not with the ideal of non-violence.

WR: I fully agree that if you see the fact, we must handle that.

K: Therefore there is no progress.

WR: That is just a word you can use any way.

K: No, not any way. When I have an ideal, to achieve that ideal I need time. Right? Therefore I will evolve to that. So no ideals—only facts.

WR: That is perfectly so. What is the difference, what is the argument? We agree that there are only facts.

K: Which means, sir, that to look at facts time is not necessary.

WR: Absolutely not.

K: Therefore, if time is not necessary, I can see it now.

WR: Yes, certainly.

K: You can see it now. Why don't you?

WR: Why don't you? That is another question.

K: No, not another question.

DB: If you take it seriously that time is not necessary, one could perhaps clear up the whole thing right now.

WR: Yes, that does not mean all human beings can do it, there are people who can do it.

K: No, if I can see it, you can see it.

WR: I don't think so, I don't agree with you.

K: It is not a question of agreement or disagreement. But when we have ideals away from facts, time, progress, are necessary to get there. I must have knowledge to progress. All that comes in, right? So can you abandon ideals?

WR: It is possible.

K: Ah, no, the moment you use the word "possible," time is there!

WR: I mean seeing the fact is possible.

K: Do it now, sir—forgive me, I am not being authoritarian— when you say, "It is possible," you have already moved away.

WR: I mean to say, I must say, that not everybody can do it.

K: How do you know?

WR: That is a fact.

K: No, I won't accept that.

IS: Perhaps I can come in with a concrete example. If I stand on a high springboard over a swimming pool and I cannot swim, and I am told, "Just jump in and relax completely and the water will carry you," that is perfectly true, I can do it. There is nothing that prevents me except that I am frightened of doing it. That is, I think, the issue. Of course we can do it, there is no difficulty, but there is this basic fear, which does not stand to reason, that makes us shy away.

K: Please forgive me, I am not talking of that, we are not saying that. But if one realizes that one is greedy, why do we invent non-greed?

IS: I wouldn't know, because it seems to me so obvious that if I am greedy, then I am greedy.

K: So why do we have the opposite? Why? All the religions say we must not be greedy, all the philosophers, if they are worth their salt, say, Don't be greedy, or something else. Or they say, If you are greedy you will not reach heaven. So they have always culti- vated through tradition, through saints, the whole gamut, this idea of the opposite. So I don't accept that. I say *that* is an escape from *this*.

IS: Which it is. It is at best a halfway stage.

K: It is an escape from this, right? And it won't solve this problem. So to deal with the problem, to remove it, I can't have one foot there and one foot here. I must have both my feet here.

IS: And if both my feet are here?

K: Wait, that is a simile, a simile. So I have no opposite that implies time, progress, practicing, trying, becoming, the whole gamut of that.

IS: So I see I am greedy or I am violent.

K: Now we have to go into something entirely different. Can a human being be free of greed *now*? That's the question. Not eventually. You see, I am not interested in not being greedy next life, or the day after tomorrow, who cares? I want to be free of sorrow, pain, now. So I have no ideals at all. Right, sir? Then I have only this fact: I am greedy. What is greed? The very word is condemnatory. The word "greed" has been in my mind for centuries, and the word immediately condemns the fact. By saying, "I am greedy," I have already condemned it. Now can I look at that fact without the word with all its intimations, its content, and its tradition? Look at it. You cannot understand the depth of the feeling of greed or be free of it if you are caught in words. So as my whole being is concerned with greed, it says, "All right, I won't be caught in it, I won't use the word 'greed.'" Right? Now, is that feeling devoid of the word, divorced from the word "greed"?

IS: No, it isn't, please go on.

K: So as my mind is full of words and caught in words, can it look at something, "greed," without the word?

WR: That is really seeing the fact.

K: Then only do I see the fact, then only do I see the fact.

WR: Yes, without the word.

K: Therefore it has no value, it's finished. This is where the difficulty lies, sir. I want to be free of greed because everything in my blood, my tradition, my upbringing, my education, says, Be free of that ugly thing. So all the time I am making an effort to be free of it. Right? I was not educated, thank God, on those lines. So I say all right, I have only the fact, the fact is that I am greedy. I want to understand the nature and structure of that word, of that feeling. What is it? What is the nature of that feeling? Is it a remembrance? If it is a remembrance, I am looking at the present greed with past remembrances. The past remembrances have said, condemn it. Can I look at it without past remembrances?

I'll go into this a little more, because the past remembrance condemns greed and therefore strengthens it. If it is something new, I won't condemn it. But because it is not, it is new but made old by remembrances, memories, experience, I condemn it. So can I look at it without the word, without the association of words? That doesn't need discipline or practice, that doesn't need a guide. Just this—can I look at it without the word? Can I look at that tree, woman, man, sky, heaven, or bird without the word and find out? But if someone comes along and says, "I'll show you how to do it," then I am lost. And "how to do it" is the whole business of the sacred books—sorry—all the gurus, the bishops, the popes, the whole of that.

Is There a State of Mind
without the Self?

*Second Conversation with the Buddhist Scholars
Walpola Rahula and Irmgard Schloegl, and with
Professor David Bohm and Others*

WALPOLA RAHULA: I would like to ask you to clarify one or two things. When we concluded our discussion yesterday, you were saying that the idea of greed being something bad is conveyed by the word itself, but that if you see it without the word it may not be the same thing. And of course that is quite right, because the thing itself has no word when you really see the thing. In Buddhist terminology there are three levels of knowledge. One level is when we acquire wisdom and self-knowledge through learning, books, and the teacher, called *shrutamaya-prajna*. Then there is further development, the wisdom that you get by thinking, by meditating according to that knowledge, which is still within words, still within language, that is *chintamaya-prajna*. But the highest wisdom goes beyond words, and has no words, no name, no terminology, that is *bhavanamaya-prajna.* That means that you see the thing without a word. I think that is what you meant when you said that when you see the thing, all our reflections, and our accumulated meanings, disappear. That was my understanding. I don't know whether that is what you meant.

KRISHNAMURTI: Perhaps we will go into it, sir, but you also said you would like to ask some other questions.

WR: That's right. I am very grateful to you. These questions have been on my mind for a long time. Sir, you know the word *arahant* in Buddhist terminology. An arahant is a person who has realized the truth, who is liberated, who is free. It is a very well known term. And the disciples of the Buddha, and various other people, often asked him what happens to an arahant after his death. Someone asked, "Does he exist after his death?" And the Buddha said, "No." "Then can one say he does not exist?" The Buddha said, "No." "Then he exists and does not exist?" The Buddha said, "No." "Then he does not exist, nor not exist?" "The Buddha said, "No, none of those terms, 'exist' or 'does not exist,' 'is' or 'is not,' can be applied to that state." These are called the four *kotis* or extremes. And all these terms, which are relative and dualistic, are used only within our knowledge, our experience, within the empirical world. But this state is beyond that world, therefore you can't apply any of these words. This question was put repeatedly to the Buddha, and that was his answer. What do you say to this? The Buddha said, "You cannot say he exists or does not exist."

K: Sir, could we talk over together what is living and what is dying, and what is the state of the mind that is dead, or in the process of dying? Could my putting it that way help to answer the question?

WR: I don't know.

K: You see, after all, the arahant is known also, I believe, in

Hindu thought. Not that I have read any books about this, but I have discussed it with people. Human beings throughout the world, as far as one can make out, are always inquiring into or having beliefs about death, asking if there is life after death, whether there is a continuity. And if there is no continuity what is the point of living at all? Life is such a dreadful affair anyhow, with a lot of trouble, anxiety, fear, so if there is no reward for living properly, correctly, what is the point of being good, kind, noble, and so on? Could we approach your question from that point of view? Or do you want to ask what is the state of a mind that has no self whatsoever?

WR: That's right, that is the state of an arahant.

K: That is what I want to get at. Could we go into it that way?

WR: I think that is a good approach, because the arahant has no self whatsoever.

K: Is that possible? I am not saying it is or is not, we are inquiring, proceeding through exploring and finding out, not believing or disbelieving. So what is the self? The name, the form, the body, the organism. The name identifies itself with the body, certain characteristics identifying themselves with the "me"—I am strong, I am weak, I have got a good character, I am not bad. So the characteristic, the tendency, is identified by thought as the "me." The experiences, the accumulated knowledge, as identified by thought as the "me," and the "me" is that which I possess—my property, my house, my furniture, my wife, my books. All that, the violence, the pleasure, the fear, the agonies, together with the name, the form, constitutes the self. So what is the root of the self? Is the root of the self the acquired experiences? I am inquiring—we are inquiring—into the very root of it, not the mere expressions of it. So the whole process of identification—my house, my name, my possessions, what I will be, the success, the power, the position, the prestige—the process of identification is the essence of the self. If there is no identification, is there the self? You understand, sir?

WR: Yes, I follow.

K: So can this identification, which is the movement of thought, come to an end? If thought didn't say that is my furniture, identifying itself with that, because it gives pleasure, position, and security, all that, there would be no identification. So the root of the self is the movement of thought.

WR: Yes.

K: So death is the ending of that movement. Or is death a continuity of that movement into the next life? You understand?

WR: Quite.

K: Why should the arahant, or the liberated man, wait until the end, till he reaches that which is called death? We realize that the very root of the self is the movement of thought in time, in distance, from here to there, and all the conflicts, miseries, confusions created by thought are the self. So when thought comes to an end that is a form of death while living.

WR: Yes.

K: Now, can thought come to an end? To bring that about, or wanting thought to end, we meditate, we practice, we are aware, we go through all the tortures of so-called meditation. Right sir? Would you agree to that?

WR: In popular religion.

K: No, you see, if I may point out, sir, the ordinary man is not interested in all this. He wants his beer or whatever, he is not interested, perhaps because of wrong education, social conditions, economic position, environmental influences, and maybe the religions have helped to keep him down, the elite being somewhere else—the Pope, the cardinals—you follow? So I wouldn't, if I may point out, I wouldn't say "popular." It is the human tendency that we are talking about here. Every human being has identified himself, and so conditioned himself, with something or other, with God, with nirvana, with *moksha*, with heaven, with paradise and so on. Now, while living, can that death which is the end of thought take place? Not at the end of one's life, which is then a graveyard renunciation that has no meaning.

WR: I agree when you say it is not necessary to wait until the end of your life, until your death, and Buddha pointed out the same thing. When a disciple asked him what would happen to the Buddha after his death, he asked the disciple, "What is Buddha? Is it this body?" He put exactly the same questions that you have put about name and form. In Buddhist terminology it is called the *nama-rupa*.

K: In Sanskrit too.

WR: And the disciple said, "No, the Buddha is not the body." So, as one can't pinpoint even the living Buddha now, how can one do it after death?

K: Sir, if I may ask—I hope you don't think me impudent—why do we bring in the Buddha? We are talking as human beings.

WR: This was just because I raised the question from the Buddha's point of view.

K: But I as a human being want to know what happens after death, or what is the significance of death. Or can one live in daily life not as a monk, as a saint, all that stuff, without the self?

WR: Of course my question was not that. My question was: What happens to the person who has realized the truth, who has become liberated, free?

K: I would never ask that question, because one might say this happens, or one might say that happens, or that nothing happens. Then it becomes a theory to me, which is an idea.

WR: I wanted from you a little more than that.

K: Ah, you wanted from me . . .

WR: Not a theory.

K: If you want it from this person who is talking, you have to inquire as he is inquiring. And he is asking, Is it possible, not at the end of one's existence, but in daily life, to live without this process of identification that is the result of thought and which brings about the structure and nature of the self? Can the movement of thought end while I am living? That is the question, rather than what happens when I die. The "me" is merely a movement of thought. And thought itself is very limited. It is a small, broken-up piece in a vast movement. And so long as thought is limited, a broken-up thing, a fragment, whatever it creates will still be limited, broken-up, and fragmentary. Right? So can a human being, you or I or any of us, can we live without the movement of thought which is the essence of the self? Suppose I say, Yes, it can be done—what value has it for you?

IRMGARD SCHLOEGL: Once that identification of thought and "me" is really broken . . .

K: No, not broken, end.

IS: That is what I mean, end.

K: When you break something it can continue. It is an ending.

IS: It can never come back in the same way, it is an irrevocable ending.

K: All I am saying is, suppose the speaker, this person says, Yes, it is possible, I know it is possible, then what? What value has it for you?

IS: Personally, that is what I hope we can discuss.

K: I am coming to that. What value has that for you? Either you accept it, or you say, Don't be silly, it's not possible, and walk away. But if you want to inquire and say, Look, let's find out if it is possible—not as an idea, but as an actuality in daily life . . . [*looking around at the audience*] Somebody else join in!

GIDDU NARAYAN: Dr. Rahula, we have been talking in this context of the value of Buddhist meditation, preparation, practice, and mindfulness. What is the value of all those things that are mentioned in the Buddhist literature, which are practiced as very important in relation to the ending of thought?

WR: The ending of thought or of the self?

GN: The role of mindfulness, *satipatthana*, let us say.

WR: Mindfulness, or rather presence of awareness—a sense of mindfulness. Yes, *satipatthana* has many aspects, but the most important one is mindfulness, awareness in everything. Even what we do here now is a meditation, it is not sitting cross-legged like a statue under a tree or in a cave, that is not meditation, that is only an external exercise. Many people regard that as meditation. They would not think that what we are doing here is meditating, but to me this is the deepest sort of meditation. *Satipatthana* also includes what is called *dharmanupashyana*, which means to see, follow, observe, or be aware of various subjects, topics, doctrines, the intellectual side of things. Then there is also meditation that is mindful of everything that you do, whatever it is, eating, drinking, or going about, talking, everything is mindfulness. And all that leads to what he says.

GN: It leads to?

WR: To ending the thought process of self.

GN: That is what I really want to get at.

K: Sir, I hope you don't think me impudent or irreverent toward what the Buddha has said. I personally haven't read any of these things, and I don't want to read anything about all this. They may be correct or not correct, they may be illusory or not illusory, they may have been put together by disciples, and what the disciples do with their gurus is appalling—everything gets twisted. So I say, Look, I don't want to start with somebody telling me what to do or what to think. I have no authority. I say, Look, as a human being who is suffering, going through agonies, sex, mischief, terror, and all the rest of it, in inquiring into all that I come to the point, which is thought. That's all. I don't have to know all the literature in the world, which will only condition further thinking. So forgive me for putting it this way, I brush all that aside. We have done this—I have met Christians, Benedictine monks, Jesuits, great scholars, always quoting, quoting, quoting, believing this is so, this is not so. You understand, sir? I hope you don't think I am irreverent.

WR: Not at all. I fully agree with you, and that is also my attitude. I am talking in order to examine it.

K: You see I only start with what for me is a fact. What is a fact, not something according to some philosopher or religious teacher or priest—a fact—I suffer, I have fear, I have sexual demands. How am I to deal with all these tremendously complex things, which make up my life where I am so utterly miserable and unhappy? I start from there, not from what somebody else has said, that means nothing. You follow, sir? Forgive me, I am not belittling the Buddha, I wouldn't do that.

WR: That I know. I know you have the highest respect for the Buddha. We have the same attitude, and I want to examine it with you. That is why I put the question.

K: No, sir, not quite, forgive me for saying so, not quite. I start with something that is common to all of us. Not according to the Buddha, not according to the Christian God or some Hindu god or some group, to me all that is totally irrelevant, they have no place, because I suffer, and I want to find out if it can be ended, or must I carry on for the rest of my life with this agony, this brutality, these sexual perversions or sexual desires, you know, all the rest of it. Right, sir? So I see that the root of all this confusion, uncertainty, insecurity, travail, effort, the root of this is the self, the "me." Now is it possible to be free of the "me," which produces all this chaos, both outwardly, politically, religiously, economically, and all the rest of it, and also inwardly, this constant struggle, constant battle, constant effort? So I am asking, can thought end? So that thought has no future—that which ends then has a totally different beginning—not the beginning of the ending of the "me" and then it picking up again later. Right, sir?

In what manner can that thought end? That's the problem. The Buddha must have talked about it. I don't think Christianity, as far as I know, has touched on this point. They said, give yourself to God, to Christ, abandon yourself to him. But the self goes on. They haven't gone into this at all, only the Hindus and the Buddhists have done so, and perhaps some others. So can this thought end? Then the priest or guru comes along and says, Yes it can end, only identify yourself with Christ, with the Buddha—you follow? Identify, forget yourself.

WR: That is the Christian attitude.

K: Christian, also part of the Hindu.

WR: But not the Buddhist one. I must defend it.

K: I know.

GN: I believe a great deal of Buddhist thought has degenerated into this.

WR: Yes, of course, there are various schools of thought, but what I am saying is in accordance with the Buddha's teaching.

K: You see . . .

IS: Shall we say it is human nature to lean on something, and this is what automatically happens, and this is what we are trying to get away from?

K: So here I am, an ordinary human being, fairly well educated, not according to schools, colleges, but fairly well educated, who has observed what the world is going through, and he says, "I am the world, I am not different from the world, because I suffer, I have created this monstrous world, my parents, my grandparents, everybody's parents, have created this." Right, sir? So how is it possible for thought to end? Some people say it is, by meditating, controlling, suppressing.

IS: No.

K: Wait, I said *some* people. Some people have said, Suppress it, identify the self with the highest, which is still the movement of thought. Some people have said, Burn out all the senses. They have done it, they fast, do everything for this thing. So somebody like me comes along and says that effort is the very essence of the self. Right? Do we understand that? Or has it become an idea, and we carry that idea out? You understand what I am talking about? I don't know if I am making myself clear.

GN: If you say effort is the very essence of the self, is there again a preparation, an initial training, to come to *that* realization? Or does one come to it effortlessly?

IS: If I have understood you, and please correct me if not, you mean that the very effort that I make to come to it, that in itself is already contributing to my delusion?

K: To the maker of the effort, who has already identified with something greater and is making an effort to reach it, it is still the movement of thought.

IS: And it is still a bargaining—if I do this, or give this up, then I will get that.

K: So how do you, if I may ask, listen? How do you listen?

IS: Listen?

K: A person like me says, effort of any kind only strengthens the self. Now, how do you receive that statement?

IS: I am entirely in agreement.

K: No, not agreement or disagreement. How do you listen to it?

IS: Let it impinge.

K: No.

DAVID BOHM: Do we listen in the same way that we have made identifications, that is in general we listen through the past, through our previous ideas, through what we know?

IS: If one can open up and just listen.

K: Ah, no. When you eat, you are eating because you are hungry. The stomach receives the food, there is no idea of receiving the food. So can you listen—listen—without the *idea* of receiving, or accepting, or denying, or arguing, just listen to a statement? It may be false, it may be true, but just listen to it. Can you do it?

IS: I would say yes.

K: Then if you listen like that, what takes place?

IS: Nothing.

K: No, madam, don't immediately say "Nothing." What takes place? I listen to a statement that thought is the root of the self, after a careful explanation of the movement of thought that identifies itself with the form, name, with this and that, and the other thing. So after explaining this very carefully, it is said that thought is the very root of the self. Now how do you receive or listen to the truth of that fact, that thought is the root of the self? Is it an idea, a conclusion, or is it an absolute, irrevocable fact?

WR: If you ask me, it is a fact. I listen to it, receive it, I see it.

K: Are you listening as a Buddhist? Forgive me for putting it that way!

41

WR: I don't know.

K: No, you must know!

WR: I am not identifying with anything at all. I am not listening to you as a Buddhist or as a non-Buddhist.

K: I am asking you, sir, are you listening as a Buddhist, as a person who has read a great deal about the Buddha, and what the Buddha has said, and so comparing—just a minute—and so you have gone away from listening? So are you listening?—I am not being personal, sir, forgive me—are you listening?

WR: Oh, you can be quite free with me—I won't misunderstand you and you won't misunderstand me. I have no fear of that.

K: No, I don't mind you misunderstanding me at all, I can correct it. [*laughter*] Are you listening to the idea, to the words, and the implications of those words, or are you listening without any sense of verbal comprehension, which you have gone through quickly, and you say, Yes, I see the absolute truth of that?

WR: That is what I have said.

K: Do you?

WR: Yes.

K: Sir, then it is finished. It is like seeing something tremendously dangerous, it is over, you don't touch it. I wonder if you see that.

DB: It seems to me there is a tendency to listen through the word, as you put it, and that word identifies, and that identification still goes on while one thinks one is listening. This is the problem, and it is very subtle.

WR: In other words, it is listening in the same way as when the word interferes in seeing, in that sense.

K: No, sir, I listen. When you say something to me, what the Buddha has said, I listen. I say, He is just quoting from what the Buddha has said, but he is not saying something I want to know. You are telling me about the Buddha, but I want to know what *you* think, not what Buddha thought, because then we are establishing a relationship between you and me, and not between you, the Buddha, and me. I wonder if you see that?

WR: That means you were also listening with another thought.

K: I was listening to what you were saying about the Buddha. I was just listening. I don't know. You are quoting and probably what you are quoting is perfectly so, you are quoting correctly and so on, but you are not revealing yourself to me, and I am revealing myself to you. Therefore we have a relationship through the Buddha, not a direct relationship. I love my dog and you like that dog too, but your liking of that dog means our relationship is based on that dog. I don't know if I am making myself clear—I am not comparing Buddha to the dog!

IS: What you are looking for is our personal, experiential response to that statement.

K: No, your "personal" experience is also the experience of everybody else; it is not personal.

IS: Though it is individually rendered.

K: If you and I suffer, it is suffering, not my suffering and your suffering. But when there is identification with suffering, then it is "my" suffering, and I say, I must be free of it. But as human beings in the world we suffer—we are going off somewhere else . . .

DB: It seems to me that this question of identification is the main one. It is very subtle, and in spite of all that you have said, identification still goes on.

K: Of course.

DB: It seems to be built into us.

IS: And this raises the question whether that identification can be ended.

DB: Identification prevents listening freely, openly, because one listens through the identification.

K: What does identification mean? Why do human beings identify themselves with something—my car, my house, my wife, my children, my country, my God, my whatever? Why?

IS: To be something, perhaps?

K: Let's inquire why. Not only identifying with outward things, but also identifying inwardly with my experience, so it is then "my" experience. Why do human beings go through this all the time?

DB: At one stage you said we identify with our sensations—for example, with our senses—and this seems very powerful. What would it be to *not* identify with our sensations?

K: Yes. So when one listens, am I listening to identify myself with that fact about which he is talking, or is there no identification at all, and therefore I am capable of listening with a totally different ear? Am I hearing just with my ears, or am I hearing with total attention? You understand, sir? Am I listening with total attention? Or is my mind wandering off and saying, "Oh my goodness, this is rather boring, and what is he or she talking about?"— and so I am off. But can I attend so completely that there is only the act of listening and nothing else, no identification, no saying, "Yes, that's a good idea, that's a bad idea, that's true, that's false," which are all processes of identification. Can I listen without any of those movements? When I do so listen, then what? The truth that thought is the essence of the self, and the self creates all this misery, is finished. I don't have to meditate, I don't have to practice, all that is over because I see the danger of this thing. So can we listen so completely that there is the absence of the self? Can I see, observe something without the self—that sky, a beautiful sky—and all the rest of that?

So the ending of thought, which is the ending, or cutting the very root, of the self—a bad simile, but take it—when there is such active, non-identifying attention, then does the self exist? I need a suit, why should there be identification in getting a suit? I get it, there is getting it. So active listening implies listening to the senses. Right, sir? To my taste, for example, the whole sensory movement. You can't stop the senses, then you would be paralyzed. But the moment I say, "That's a marvelous taste, I must have more of that," the whole identification begins.

DB: It seems to me that to be identifying with the senses is the general condition of mankind. Now, how are we going to change that?

K: Of course, that is the whole problem, sir. Humankind has been educated, conditioned for millennia to identify with everything—my guru, my house, my God, my country, my king, my queen, and all that horrible business that goes on.

DB: With each one of those there is a sensation.

K: It is a sensation, which you call experience.

WR: So we should come to our point.

K: Yes, which is?

WR: The one that we began with.

K: Yes, death. When the self ends—it can end, obviously, except for the most ignorant, and for people highly burdened with knowledge, who identify themselves with knowledge and all that. When there is the ending of the self, what takes place? Not at the end of my life, not when the brain is deteriorating, but when the brain is highly active, quiet, alive, what then takes place, when the self is not? Now, how can you find out, sir? Say X has ended the self completely, doesn't pick it up again in the future, on another day, but ends it *completely*. He says, Yes, there is a totally different activity that is not the self. What good is that to me, or to any of us? He says, Yes, it can end, there is a different world altogether, in a different dimension, not a sensory dimension, not an intellectually projected dimension, but something totally different. I say he must either be cuckoo, a charlatan, or a hypocrite, but I want to find out, not because he says so, but because I want to find out. Can I, as a human being living in this tremendously ugly, brutal, violent world, economically, socially, morally and all the rest of it, live without the self? I want to find out. And I want to find out not as an idea, I want to do it, it is my passion. Then I begin to inquire: Why is there identification with the form, with the name—it is not very important whether you are K or W or Y. So you examine this very, very carefully—not to identify yourself with anything, with sensation, with ideas, with a country, with an experience. You understand, sir?

Can you do it? Not vaguely and occasionally, but as something that you have got to do with passion, with intensity, to find out. That means I must put everything in its right place. I have to live, to have food, but I don't have to identify myself with this or that food, I eat the correct food, and it's finished, therefore it has its right place. There are all the bodily demands, sex, to put in their right place. Who will tell me to put them in the right place? My guru, the Pope, a scripture? If they do, I identify myself with them because they are helping me to put things in the right place, which is sheer nonsense. Right, sir? The Pope can't tell me sex has its right place. He says: Marry, don't divorce, your marriage is with God, all that. And I am stuck. Why should I obey the Pope, or the guru, or scripture, or the politicians? So I have to find out what the right place is, for sex, or money. How shall I find out what is the right place for sex, which is one of the most powerful, urgent, physical demands, which the religious people say cut out, destroy, suppress, take a vow against it, and all the rest of it. I say, sorry, that doesn't mean a thing to me. So I want to find out what is its right place. How shall I find out?

I have got the key to it. The key is nonidentification with sensation. Right, sir? So nonidentification with sensation, which is translated into the modern word "experience"—I must experience sex. Right? Identification with sensation makes the self. So is it possible not to identify with sensation? There are sensations, I am hungry, but sex is a little more powerful. So I have got the key to it, the truth of it. So, I feel sexual, all right. Nonidentification, that is the truth of it. If I really see that truth, then sex, money, everything has its right place.

WR: In other words—may I put it this way?—you see without the self.

K: Ah, no.

WR: Identification is self.

K: No, there is the truth that identification with sensation, with this or that, builds the structure of the self. Right? Is that an absolute, irrevocable, passionate, lasting truth? Or is it just an idea which I have accepted as true, and I can change that idea tomorrow? But this thing is irrevocable. One must have money—and money gives you freedom to do what you like, sex, if you want it, money enables you to travel, gives you a sense of power, position—you know, all the rest of it. So nonidentification with money. You follow?

DB: And that means the end of desire for anything.

K: No, in the end desire has very little meaning. But it doesn't mean I am a dead vegetable.

DB: Are you saying identification gives desire excessive meaning?

K: Of course. So having put everything in its right place—I don't put it, it happens because I have seen the truth of this thing—everything falls into its right place. Right? No, I can't say that is right or wrong.

WR: No, I see what you are saying.

K: Then what place has thought? Has it any place at all? Obviously, when I am talking I am using words, the words are associated with memory and so on, so there is thinking there—not with me, there is very little thinking as I am talking, but don't let's go into that. So thought has a place. When I have to catch a train, when I have to go to the dentist, when I go to do something, thought has its place. And it has no place psychologically in the identifying process. Right? I wonder if you see.

GN: Are you implying that, because there is no thought, the identifying process has lost its strength?

K: No, it hasn't lost its strength.

GN: Or it doesn't happen at all.

K: No, we said just now that having the key, or living with the fact, living with the truth that identification brings about the structure and nature of the self, which creates all the innumerable problems, seeing and living that truth—living it, it's in my breath, my throat, my gullet, it's part of my blood seeing the truth of that, that truth is there. And then thought has its right place. I put money, sex—not "I" . . .

IS: They fall into their right place.

K: Now I want to go further into this.

GN: If the insight, the passion, the truth, is powerful . . .

K: No, you see you are using the word "powerful."

GN: Yes, I am using it.

K: No, it is not powerful.

GN: It has its own strength.

K: No, you can't use those words.

GN: If it has no strength, thought asserts itself.

K: No, it is not strength.

DB: You are saying that it is the identification that makes thought do all the wrong things.

K: That's right, identification has made thought do the wrong things.

DB: It would be all right otherwise.

K: Otherwise thought has its place.

DB: But when you say no identification, then you mean the self is empty, that it has no content?

K: There are only sensations.

DB: There are sensations, but they are not identified.

K: Not identified.

GN: Through thought.

K: Not identified!

DB: They are just going on, do you mean?

K: Yes, sensations are going on.

DB: Outside or inside.

K: Inside.

GN: And you are also implying there is no slipping back.

K: Of course not. When you see something most dangerous, you don't slip back or go forward, it is dangerous! Now, to go back to the question we began with. Is that death? Death, as we know it, means that the brain cells and so forth die. Right? The body deteriorates, there is no oxygen, and all the rest of it. So it dies, and sensations die with it.

DB: Sensations, you say, die with the body. So there is no sensation.

K: No sensation. Now, is there a living with the sensations

49

being fully awakened? They are awakened, they are alive, but the non-identifying with sensations wipes away the self. We have said that. Now what is death? Is it possible to live a daily life with death, which is the ending of the self?

WR: Yes.

K: Go on, somebody else talk for a while.

WR: I follow what you are saying.

GN: Would you say there is a great deal of talk about insight—insight meditation, *vipassana*—in Buddhism? Is insight a thing we can use, and which doesn't slip back? Is insight of that quality?

WR: Insight meditation is exactly what Krishnaji is now referring to.

GN: No, I am asking, does insight endure without reference to time?

K: Don't use the words "endure," "last."

GN: All insight is a momentary process.

K: The moment you have an insight, it is finished.

WR: Once you see it, it is finished.

K: I have an insight into the whole nature of the self.

WR: That is exactly what he is saying.

GN: It is complete, otherwise it is not insight.

WR: In itself it is complete and there is no coming back. You have seen it and you know it.

IS: Who has seen it? With those words we always get into trouble.

WR: No, this is only the language. There is no seer apart from seeing.

DB: Would you say that the insight transforms the person?

K: That is what we were discussing the other day—the insight transforms not only the state of the mind, but the brain cells themselves undergo a change.

WR: Absolutely.

DB: Therefore the brain cells, being in a different state, behave differently; it is not necessary to repeat the insight.

WR: The whole system changes with that.

K: Be careful, sir, don't—either it is so, or it is not. So I am left with this now. I am left with the question of what is death. Is the ending of the self death? It is not, obviously, in the ordinary accepted sense of the word "death," because the blood is circulating, the brain is working, the heart is pumping, and all the rest of it.

DB: It is still alive.

K: It is alive, but the self is nonexistent because there is no identification of any kind. This is a tremendous thing. Nonidentification with anything, with experience, with belief, with a country, with ideas, ideals, wife, husband, love, no identification at all. Is that death? People who hear death called that say, My God, if I don't identify myself with my something or other, I am nothing. So they are afraid of being nothing, and then identify. But nothingness, which is not a thing, you understand, sir, not a thing, it is therefore quite a different state of mind. Now that is death. Death while there is living, sensations, the heart beating, the blood circulating, breathing, the brain active, undamaged. Our brains are damaged.

DB: Well, is it possible to heal the damage?

K: With insight, that is what I want to get at. Our brains are damaged. For thousands of years we have been hurt psychologically, inwardly, and that hurt is part of our brain cells, remembered hurts, the propaganda for two thousand years that I am a Christian, that I believe in Jesus Christ, which is a hurt. Or I am a

Buddhist—you follow, sir—that is a hurt. So our brains are damaged. To heal that damage is to listen very carefully, to listen, and in the listening to have an insight into what is being said, and therefore there is immediately a change in the brain cells. Therefore a complete and total absence of identification. And is that then love? You see I've questioned this, sir. There is great talk about compassion, isn't there, in the Buddhist literature. Be compassionate, don't kill, don't hurt. What place has love in compassion? To love a man or a woman, or a dog, or a piece of stone, a stray cat, to love something, the clouds, the trees, or nature, anything, to love the house put together by architects, a beautiful thing, the bricks. To love it, which is non-identifying with the house, the bricks. The dying while living—is that love?—in which there is no attachment.

WR: That is so.

K: So then what place has love? Loving a woman, a man—not identifying, please, with the sensations of sex with a woman or with a man, and yet to love that person. When there is that love, that love is not the woman whom I love, it is global love. I wonder if you see.

WR: Fully.

K: Don't agree, sir.

WR: No, not agree, I see it.

K: What place has that quality with compassion? Or is compassion the same as love?

WR: No.

GN: Why do you say no?

WR: Compassion is only for people suffering. With love, there is no discrimination, whereas compassion is directed toward those who are suffering.

GN: Buddhist terminology makes a distinction between compassion and love?

WR: Yes, *karuna* is compassion, and love is *maitri*, it is more than compassion.

K: Sir, does one love without identification, which implies no self, no attachment?

WR: That is true love.

K: No, I am asking you, as a human being, not as a Buddhist, but as a human being. Do you, without identifying with your senses and so on, love a woman or a man, or a child, or the sky or a stone, or a stray dog? Without identifying? They all suffer—the woman suffers, the man suffers, a stray dog has a terrible life, chased and kicked. And when there is no identification, do you love that dog, or do you have compassion for that dog? Is compassion an idea—I must have compassion for the suffering, for the poor, for the demented?

DB: I still think the question is, is there love for somebody who is not suffering? Suppose there is somebody who is not suffering.

K: Suppose somebody is frightfully happy, because he writes good books, or thrillers, and gets a lot of money, has a jolly good life.

DB: I didn't mean that exactly. You could say that he was suffering underneath.

K: That's what I am questioning.

DB: But would there be love if there were no suffering? You know, if mankind were to be free of it.

K: Would there be love without suffering? Or are you saying a human being must go through suffering to have love?

DB: Well, not necessarily.

K: You see, when you put it that way, that is what it implies, doesn't it?

DB: Well, one view is that there could be love whether there is suffering or not. And the other view is that compassion, the way the Buddhists use it, is only for suffering.

K: I question that.

GN: I didn't quite feel that *karuna*, compassion, was only for those who were suffering. I think it has a wider quality than that.

WR: No, there are four qualities called *brahma-viharas*, the supreme qualities—*maitri*, *karuna*, *mudita*, *upeksha*. *Maitri* embraces both suffering and not suffering, *karuna* embraces only suffering, *mudita* is directed toward happy people, sympathetic joy in their happiness—in the world there is no such joy—and *upeksha* is equanimity. These four qualities are called the *brahma-viharas*, the supreme, divine qualities. Compared with that classification, your use of the word "love" means something much greater.

K: I haven't come to compassion yet, sir. I just want to know as a human being, do I love somebody—the dog, the chimney, the clouds, that beautiful sky, without identifying? Not as a theory, but as a *fact*. I don't want to delude myself with theories or ideas, I want to know if I love that man or woman or child or dog or house without saying, "It is my dog, my wife, my son, my house, my bricks." Actually, not as abstractions.

IS: Yes, if identification with the "I" is gone, but as long as I feel the "I" is acting as self, I cannot do it.

K: No, madam. We said the truth is that identification breeds the self which causes all the trouble, the misery.

IS: And if that is seen . . .

K: I have said that, it is an absolute, irrevocable reality, it is in my blood. I can't get rid of my blood, it is there.

IS: Then I cannot help but love.

K: You are all too quick! Not "I cannot help loving"—but *do* you?

WR: If you see it.

K: No. Do you *see* the truth, the truth of that, that identification is the root of the self, with thought and all the rest of it? So that it is an absolute fact, like a cobra, like a dangerous animal, like a precipice, like taking deadly poison. So there is absolutely no identification, when you see the danger. Then what is my relationship to the world, to nature, to my woman, man, child? When there is no identification, is there indifference, callousness, brutality—you just say, "I don't identify," and put your nose in the air?

WR: That would be a very selfish attitude.

K: No, not selfish. Is this what is going to happen?

WR: No.

K: You can't just say no. Why not? It will happen, if it is intellectual.

IS: If it is intellectual, it is not truth.

K: If I have an ideal.

WR: That is what I have said, then you have not seen.

K: No, what I am asking, sir, is this. Is nonidentification an ideal, a belief, an idea that I am going to live with, and therefore my relationship to the dog, the wife, the husband, the girl, or whatever, becomes very superficial and casual? It is only when the truth is that identification is absolutely cut out of one's life that there is no callousness—because that is real.

We haven't solved the question of death yet. It is five minutes past one, and we have to stop for lunch.

WR: And in the afternoon I have some more questions, a list of things.

K: Good, let's go through them then.

Free Will, Action, Love, and Identification and the Self

Third Conversation with the Buddhist Scholars
Walpola Rahula and Irmgard Schloegl, and with
Professor David Bohm and Others

GIDDU NARAYAN: I suggest that Dr. Rahula puts all the questions that he has noted down, so that we can cover most of the ground. And I have also got one or two questions.

WALPOLA RAHULA: Why not put your questions first?

GN: My question is about the Buddhist Mahayana philosophy developed by Nagarjuna in the second century. Probably the greatest Buddhist thinker, he talked a great deal about *shunyata*, or voidness, which is very closely associated with insight. And I believe that the whole of later Buddhist thought owes its strength to Nagarjuna's idea of *shunyata* as being something which is pure, which is pristine. I will put it this way. There is no insight without *shunyata*. He said, too, that without understanding the outer there

is no possibility of going to the inner. And he also made a statement that seems fallacious: samsara is nirvana, and nirvana is
samsara.

KRISHNAMURTI: Sir, you are using Sanskrit words, perhaps
some of us may understand each other but you must explain them
very carefully.

GN: Samsara is worldly life with all its travail and suffering,
with all its sorrow—*dukkha*. Nirvana is a state of freedom, bliss,
liberation. He said samsara is nirvana, and nirvana is samsara. And
this is explained by the Buddhist scholars through *paticca-samuppada*, the whole thing is interrelated, conditioned coordination.
So this has a very powerful influence over Buddhist thought today,
as I understand it. And I would like this to be examined in the
context of what we have been talking about.

K: I haven't understood the statement.

GN: The first thing is the importance of *shunyata*.

K: What do you mean by that word, *shunyata*?

WR: From the Buddhist point of view, *shunyata* literally means
voidness or emptiness.

K: Nothingness. I know that meaning.

WR: That is the literal meaning. But the significance of *shunyata* has been attributed by Western Buddhist scholars mostly to
Nagarjuna, and that is incorrect. It is the Buddha who first used
the term, and it was Nagarjuna as a great thinker, a philosopher,
who developed it into a system. Whereas Buddha said it in a very
simple way. Ananda, his closest companion and disciple, asked
him one day, "Sir, it is said the world is *shunya*, empty, what does
it mean, to what extent is it *shunya*?" He said, "Ananda, it is
without self"—he used the word *atta*, atman—"without self and
anything pertaining to self, therefore it is *shunya*." It is very clearly
explained. On many other occasions he told people, "See the

world as *shunya* and you are liberated." And these are the original statements. Nagarjuna took these ideas and developed them in his *Madhyamika-karika* commentary on the basis of *paticca-samuppada*, often called "dependent origination"—I would rather call it "conditioned genesis." In that philosophical view, everything is interdependent, relative, nothing is absolute, everything is cause and effect, and cause cannot be separated from the result, the effect—it is a continuity. And that is also time. Nagarjuna developed this philosophy very highly in a systematic teaching of *shunyata* as voidness or emptiness. And that is exactly what Krishnaji also says. There is no self, and when you see that, there is no complication, and every problem is solved. That is how I see it in relation to his explanation. Then the second thing you said—what was the second question?

GN: The relationship between the outer and the inner.

WR: That is exactly what Krishnaji and Dr. Bohm discussed as "actuality" and "truth" or "reality" and "truth" in the book *The Wholeness of Life*. These are also accepted Buddhist philosophical positions, *samvriti-satya* and *paramartha-satya*. *Samvriti-satya* is conventional truth; that is what we do, talk and eat, all these things, within duality, within relativity. You cannot say this table is false, but in another sense it is other than this. So *samvriti-satya* is the conventional truth, and *paramartha-satya* is the ultimate, absolute truth. These two also cannot be separated.

GN: That's right.

WR: Nagarjuna clearly says in one place in the *Madhyamika-karika* that one who cannot and does not see the conventional truth is incapable of arriving at the ultimate truth. The third question you raised was about nirvana and samsara. Nagarjuna says, also in the *Karika*—I remember the words even by heart—"Nirvana has no difference whatsoever from samsara and samsara has no difference whatsoever from nirvana." To clarify the word "samsara," the strict definition is the continuity of our existence. And I remember once I put this question to Krishnaji in Paris—personally, there was just the two of us . . .

K: Two wise people!

WR: I don't know! But I put to Krishnaji this great statement by Nagarjuna, which is a very interesting one to introduce here today, and asked him what he thought. To my surprise, he said, "Who is Nagarjuna?" I said, "That is your compatriot"—because he was supposed to be from Andhra. And then I explained who Nagarjuna was historically, as a thinker and a philosopher. I said he is perhaps the boldest thinker in the history of Buddhism. Then he asked me what his attainments were. I said that we don't know, we know only his writings and writings about him, but as for his attainments, his spiritual realizations, we can't say anything. Krishnaji paused for a moment and asked me, "What did the Buddha say about all this?" I said, "Nothing." You said, "That is correct, that is right. Because I was always doubtful about accepting Nagarjuna's statement as saying so clearly and definitely that nirvana and samsara were the same."

K: I am not quite sure that all of us have understood.

WR: Yes, will you explain this point, sir?

K: May I ask you to explain a little more? What does samskara mean, actually?

WR: Samskara is something else. "Samsara" literally means wandering, going on.

K: And samskara means?

WR: Samskara means mental construction, all our thinking process.

K: The past.

WR: It belongs to the past.

K: Yes, I understood that.

WR: Our *samskaras* are our memory, knowledge, learning, all that.

K: Like an old man going back and living in the past.

WR: But samsara is continuity, while nirvana means . . .

K: Whatever it is.

WR: Whatever it is, it is never defined in positive terms by the Buddha. Whenever someone proposed a definition he said, "No, that is not nirvana."

K: So have you asked your questions, Narayan? Now, sir, you had better put your questions too in relation to what he has said.

WR: No, my question I want to put to *you*. There are many questions, but as we don't have much time . . .

K: We have plenty of time, sir.

WR: One question is that in Western philosophy, Western thought, free will has played a very important part. According to the Buddhist philosophy that Mr. Narayan mentioned—*paticca-samuppada*, conditioned origination, cause and effect—such a thing as free will is impossible, because all our thinking, all our constructs, all our work, all our knowledge is conditioned. Therefore if there is a free will, it is free only in a relative sense and it is not absolute freedom. That is the Buddhist position. That is one question I want to put to you.

K: Let's talk it over, sir. What is will? How do you explain what will is?

WR: Will is what you decide, you want.

K: No, what is the origin, the beginning of will? I will do this, I won't do that. Now, what is the meaning of will?

WR: The meaning of will is to want to do something.

K: No. All right, let me go on then. Is it not desire?

WR: It is a desire.

K: Accentuated, heightened, strengthened desire, which we call will.

DAVID BOHM: It seems to me that we make will determined. We determine the object of desire. We say, "I am determined."

K: In that there is determination.

DB: It gets fixed there.

K: I desire that, and to achieve that I make an effort. That effort, the motive of that effort is desire. So will is desire, right?

WR: It is a form of desire.

K: Now, can desire ever be free?

WR: Quite. That is what I wanted to hear from you, because you don't like to say that, but I want to raise that.

K: Desire can never be free. It can change the objects that it has, I can desire one year to go and buy this, the next year change and desire to buy that. So desire is constant, but the objects vary. And with the strengthening of desire, I *will* do that, the will is in operation. Will is desire. Now, can desire ever be free?

WR: No.

K: But we say free will exists because I can choose between this and that, between this job and that job, I can travel—except from totalitarian states—I can go freely from England to France. So the idea of free will is cultivated with a sense that human beings are free to choose. What does that mean, to choose? I can choose between blue jeans and something else, between this car and that car, between that house and so on, but why should I choose at all? Apart from material things, apart from certain books and so on, why is there choice? I am a Catholic, I give up Catholicism and become a Zen Buddhist. And if I am a Zen Buddhist, I become something else, and I choose. Why? Why is there choice at all, which gives one the impression that I am free to choose? Right, sir? So I am asking why is there the necessity of choice at all? If I am a Catholic, and saw the whole significance of Catholicism, with its abstractions, its rituals, and dogmas, you know the whole circus of it, and I abandon that, why should I join something else? Because when I have investigated this, I have investigated all the religions. So choice must exist only when the mind is confused. When it is clear there is no choice. Is that right?

WR: I think you have answered the question.

K: I haven't fully answered it.

DB: I think that Western philosophers might not agree with you.

K: They won't agree, of course.

DB: They say that choice is not desire, that will is not desire, but will is something else. Anyway, that is my impression.

K: Yes, will is something else.

DB: Will is a free act.

K: The will is something inherited or is part of the genetic process, to will, to be.

DB: For example, I can't say I know much about it, but I think that Catholic philosophers may say that when Adam sinned, he willed wrongly, he made as it were a wrong choice and set us off on the way we've taken.

K: You see, that is a very convenient way of explaining away everything. First invent Adam and Eve, the serpent and the apple, and God, and then attribute everything to the primal crime.

WR: Yes, there is a lot of mental creation in that.

DB: I think if one observes, one can see that will is the result of desire. But I think people have the impression that will is something entirely different.

K: Yes, will is part of something sacred.

DB: That's what many people think.

K: Something derived from a divine being.

WR: According to the Western way of thinking.

K: More or less. I don't know very much about Western philosophy, but people with whom I have talked, and they may not be sufficiently well informed, have given me the impression that will is something not quite human, not quite desire, not quite something that you cultivate. It is born out of original sin, original God, and so on. But if one puts all that aside, which is theoretical, problematical, and rather superstitious, then what is will and what is choice, and what is action without choice and will? You follow? That is the problem. Is there any action that is not compounded with will? I don't know what the Buddha said about this.

GN: Would you say that insight has nothing to do with will?

K: Oh, nothing whatever to do with will, or desire, or memory.

GN: So insight is something which is free from will, and also from analysis.

WR: Yes, insight is seeing. And in that seeing there is no choice, there is no discrimination, no judgment, and no moral or immoral values. You just see.

GN: So insight is not the result of will, nor is it the result of analysis.

WR: No.

K: You see, this is becoming theoretical; you are making it so theoretical.

GN: Because through analysis . . .

K: Excuse me, sir, you are making it theoretical, you have defined it, it is not this, it is not that, and you think you have insight.

GN: No, I don't think I have insight.

K: Then why discuss it?

GN: Because we have been discussing insight.

K: No, Narayan, if I may point out, we are now talking over together action in which there is no choice, in which there is no effort as will. Is there such action? I don't know, sir.

WR: There is such an action.

K: Do you know that? Or is it a theory? Forgive me, I must be clear. I am not being impudent, I want to move away, one should move away, from theories, from ideas, from conclusions, and find out for oneself the truth of the matter, which is: Is there an action in which there is no effort of will at all, and therefore no choice? So what is correct action in which there is no will, no choice, no desire?—Because will is part of desire. To find that out, one must be very clear, mustn't one, about the nature of desire? Desire is part of sensation, and desire being part of sensation, thought identifies itself with that sensation, and through identification the "I," the ego is built up, and the ego then says, "I must," or "I will not."

So we are trying to find out if there is an action not based on the principle of ideals, on desire, on will. Not "spontaneous" action—that word is a rather dangerous word because nobody is spontaneous. One thinks one can be spontaneous, but there is no such thing, because to be spontaneous one must be totally free. So is there such action? Because most of our action has a motive. Right? And motive means movement—I want to build a house, I want that woman, or that man, I am hurt psychologically, or biologically, and my motive is to hurt back—so there is always some kind of motive in action, in what we do in daily life. So then action is conditioned by the motive. The motive is part of the identification process. So if I understand—not "I" understand—if there is a perception of the truth that identification builds the whole nature, the structure, of the self, then is there an action that doesn't spring from thought? I don't know, am I right, sir?

DB: Before we go into that, could we ask why there is identification, why it is so prevalent?

K: Why does thought identify?

DB: With sensation and other things.

K: Why is there identification with something?

DB: Especially with sensation.

K: Yes, sensation. Go on, sirs, answer it. You are all experts.

GN: Is it the very nature of thought to identify, or are there forms of thought that don't identify with sensation?

K: Narayan, why do you—if I may again ask most politely and respectfully—why do you put that question? Is it a theoretical question or an actual question? Why do you, Narayan, identify?

GN: Let me put it this way . . .

K: No, I won't put it differently.

GN: The only thing I can identify with is sensation. I have nothing else to identify with.

K: So why do you give importance to sensation? Do you say: I am a sensate being and nothing else?

GN: No.

K: Ah, that's it!

GN: If I have to identify with anything, it can only be with sensation.

DB: Is there a duality in identification? Could we make it clear?

K: In identification, as you point out, sir, there is duality, the "me"—the identifier—and the identified.

DB: Is it possible that we are trying to overcome the duality by identifying, by saying, "I am not different," when you are, or when you feel you aren't?

K: You see, I don't want to enter into the field of ideologies and theories. For me, that is of no interest. But I really want to find out—perhaps I have found out—but in investigating, talking over together, is there an action in which the self is not? In daily life, not in nirvana, when I have reached freedom and all the rest of it, I want to do it in this life, as I live. Which means I have to find out—the mind has to find out—an action which has no cause, which means no motive, an action which is not the result or effect of a series of causes and effects. When that exists, action is always bound, chained. Am I making myself clear? So is there such an action?

DB: Well, it seems to me we can't find it as long as we are identifying.

K: That's right. That's why I said as long as identification exists I can't find the answer.

DB: But why does thought identify?

K: Why does thought identify with sensations?

DB: Is that irresistible, or is it something you can put aside?

K: I don't know if that is irresistible or if it is part of sensation.

DB: How is that?

K: So let us investigate.

DB: You think that sensation is behind that?

K: Perhaps. When I say "perhaps," that word is used for the purpose of investigation, not "I don't know," but "let us investigate." So why have sensations become so important in life—sexual sensations, the sensation of power, whether occult power, or political power, economic power, or power of a woman over a man, or of a man over a woman, the power and influence, the pressures, of the environment—why has thought yielded to this pressure? Right, sir?

DB: Does sensation necessarily produce a pressure?

K: It does when it is identified.

DB: Yes, but then it is the two together.

K: I know, but let's examine. What do we mean by "sensation"?

DB: Well, we have the senses, and we may have a remembered sensation of pleasure.

K: Senses, the operation of the senses—touching, tasting, seeing, smelling, hearing.

DB: The experience that happens then, and also the memory of it.

K: No, the memory is only when there is an identification with it.

DB: I agree, yes.

K: When there is no identification, the senses are senses. But why does thought identify itself with senses?

DB: Yes, that is not yet clear.

K: We are going to make it clear.

DB: Are you saying that when the sensation is remembered, we then have identification?

K: Yes.

DB: Can we make that more clear?

K: Let's make it a little more clear. Let's work at it. There is perceiving—seeing—a pleasurable, beautiful lake. What takes place in that seeing? There is not only optical nerve seeing by the eye, but also the senses are awakened, the smell of the water, the trees by the lake . . .

DB: Could we stop a moment? When you say "seeing," of course you see through the visual sense.

K: I am using purely the visual sense.

DB: Therefore you already have the visual sense awakened merely to see. Is that what you mean?

K: Yes, just seeing. Visually, optically, I am just seeing, then what takes place?

DB: Then the other senses start to operate.

K: And the other senses start operating. Why doesn't it stop there?

DB: What is the next step?

K: The next step is thought comes in: How beautiful that is, I wish I could remain here.

DB: So thought identifies it. It says, "It is this."

K: Yes, because in that there is pleasure.

DB: In what?

K: Seeing and the delight of seeing, then thought comes into operation and says, "I must have more, I must build a house here, it is mine."

DB: But why does thought do that?

K: Why does thought interfere with the senses—is that it? Now wait a minute, sir. The moment the senses take pleasure, say, "How delightful," and stop there, thought doesn't enter. Right? Now why does thought enter? If it is painful, thought avoids it, it doesn't identify itself with that.

DB: It identifies against it, it says, "I don't want it."

K: Leave it alone, go away from it, either deny it or move away from it. But if it is pleasurable, when the senses begin to enjoy it and say, "How nice," then thought begins to identify itself with it.

DB: But why, I mean?

K: Why? Because of pleasure.

DB: But why doesn't it give it up when it sees how futile this is?

K: Oh, that's much later on. When it becomes painful, when it is aware that identification breeds both pleasure and fear, then it begins to question.

DB: Well, are you saying that thought has made a simple mistake, a kind of innocent mistake, in the beginning?

K: That's right. Thought has made a mistake in identifying with something that brings it pleasure, or where there is pleasure in something.

DB: And thought tries to take over.

K: To take over.

DB: To make it permanent, perhaps.

K: Permanent, that's right, which means memory. A remembrance of the lake with the daffodils, the trees, the water, the sunlight, and all the rest of it.

DB: I understand that thought has made a mistake, and later it discovers that mistake, but it seems to be too late, because it doesn't know how to stop.

K: It is now conditioned.

DB: So can we make it clear why it cannot give it up?

K: Why it cannot give it up. That's our whole problem.

DB: Can we try to make it more clear?

K: Why doesn't thought give up something when it knows, or is aware, that it is painful, destructive?

DB: Yes.

K: Why? Go on, why? Sir, let's take a simple example. Say that psychologically one is hurt.

DB: Well, that is later.

K: I am taking that as an example, it doesn't matter if it is later. One is hurt; why can't one immediately give up that hurt, knowing that hurt is going to create a great deal of damage? That is, when I am hurt, I build a wall around myself not to be hurt more, there is fear, isolation, neurotic action, all that follows. Thought has created the image about myself, and that image gets hurt. Why doesn't thought say, "Yes, by Jove, I have seen this," and drop it immediately? It is the same question. Because when it drops the image, there is nothing left.

DB: Then you have another ingredient, because thought wants to hold onto the memory of the image.

K: To hold on to the memories that have created the image.

DB: And which may create it again, and thought feels they are very precious.

K: Yes, they are very precious, nostalgic and all the rest of it.

DB: So somehow it gives very high value to all that. How did it come to do that?

K: Why has it made the image so valuable? Why has the image which thought has created become so important?

DB: We are saying that in the beginning it was a simple mistake. Thought made an image of pleasure and it seemed to become very important, and precious, and was unable to give it up.

K: Yes, why doesn't it? Sir, if I give up pleasure, if thought gives up pleasure, what is there left?

DB: It can't seem to return to the state in the beginning when there was nothing.

K: Ah, that is the pristine state.

DB: It is unable to return to that state.

K: It can't because thought—you know, all the rest of it.

DB: Well, I think what happens is that when thought thinks of giving up pleasure which has become very precious, then the mere thought of that is painful.

K: Yes, giving up is painful.

DB: And therefore thought runs away from that. It does not wish to face the pain.

K: Yes, so it clings to pleasure, until there is a better reward, which will be a better pleasure.

DB: But that's no change.

K: Of course not.

DB: So thought seems to have fallen into a trap, which it has done because it has innocently remembered pleasure, then gradually made that important, and then it has become too painful to give it up. Because any change from the immediate removal of pleasure is very painful.

K: Because it then has nothing else afterward, it is frightened.

DB: But you see, in the beginning it was not frightened to have nothing else.

K: Yes.

DB: Now it is.

K: Yes, in the beginning, that means the beginning of Man. Can we question even that?

DB: Perhaps not.

K: The beginning of the ape.

DB: If you go back far enough. You mean to say it has been going on a long time, but thought has built this trap that has gradually grown worse.

K: Sir, could we say that as the brain is very old—all our brains are very old—merely tracing it back further and further and further, you can never find out. But I can say that my brain is now as it is, which is very old, conditioned, in terms of pleasure and pain.

DB: They say the old brain is also the emotional product of the brain.

K: Of course, emotional, sensory and all the rest of it. So where are we now?

DB: Well, we say this brain has conditioned itself by continual memory of the image of pleasure, with the unpleasantness of giving it up, and the fear of doing so.

K: So it clings to something that it knows.

DB: Which it knows and which is very precious to it.

K: But it doesn't know that it is going to breed fear.

DB: Even when it knows it still clings.

K: But it would much rather run away from fear, hoping the pleasure will continue.

DB: But I think eventually it starts to become irrational because it creates pressures that make the brain irrational and unable to get this straight.

K: Yes. Where are we now, at the end of this? We started off, didn't we, Dr. Bohm, asking whether there is an action in which there is no motive, no cause, where the self doesn't enter at all. Of course there is. There is when the self is not, which means when no identifying process takes place. There is the perceiving of a beautiful lake with all the color, glory, and beauty of it, that is enough. Not the cultivating of memory, which is developed through the identification process. Right?

DB: This raises the question as to how we are going to stop this identification.

K: I don't think there is a "how." You see, that means meditation, control, practice, practice, practice. And that way makes the mind mechanical, dull—forgive me—and literally incapable of receiving anything new.

IRMGARD SCHLOEGL: If these practices are just imitated, this is precisely what happens.

WR: If the practice becomes imitation, then the mind is mechanical.

K: What do you mean by "imitation"?

IS: If you tell me—to make it very simple—that something will happen if you put your hand on the floor three times a day and I do it without thinking about it, without inquiring about it, without asking why, if I just mechanically do it, nothing will happen, I will only get more and more fuzzy. But if I inquire why, what for, what is my reaction . . .

K: But my question is this. Say I have listened to somebody who says, "Put your hand there," and then I begin to inquire about it. But I don't accept anybody telling me that I must put my hand there, then I don't have to inquire! Do you remember that famous story of a guru, he had a favorite cat, and he had many disciples. Every morning before they all started meditation, he put the cat on his lap and meditated. And when he died, the disciples searched around for a cat.

WR: I heard a different version. The cat had to be tied up so he could not come and disturb the meditation!

K: Same thing. You see, our minds are mechanical anyhow, have been made mechanical. Can't we investigate why we have become mechanical, rather than practice that which is non-mechanical, which may be mechanical?

IS: We can, since there have been people who have become whole before us . . .

K: I don't know.

IS: Or it seems so.

K: I don't know anybody.

IS: It seems likely.

K: You see, you accept it.

IS: Looking at it as a possible proposition.

K: I don't know. I start with myself. I don't look to somebody who is enlightened. I don't know. They may deceive themselves. So one must start with oneself. Oneself is already secondhand, living in the shadow of others, so why look to others? So here I am. From there I begin. It is so simple, whereas the other leads to so many complications.

IS: I do not necessarily see it as a complication. If I have an idea that there is something that is more than my illusion, my suffering, my general state of dissatisfaction in which I am, and which I have to face, if I do not think that there is any such possibility, then I might not even try. If I see that there might be a possibility, I do not need to take it for truth, but it gives me the sense that it is worthwhile trying to work with myself as my own subject of experiment, to work it out.

K: Why do you want a motive?

IS: I think it is almost impossible not to start with that motive, because that starts from self.

K: No, madam, we are talking about the same thing, aren't we? I just want to know myself, not because I suffer, what I go through, you know, I just want to know what I am, not according to anybody but just know about myself. So I begin to inquire, I begin to look in the mirror, which is myself. The mirror says, "Your reactions are these, and as long as you have these reactions you are going to pay heavily, you are going to suffer." So that is all. So now how am I, an ordinary human being, knowing all my reactions, ugly, pleasant, hateful, all the reactions one has, to bring about an observation in which there is no motive to restrain or to expand reactions? I wonder if I am making myself clear.

IS: Yes.

K: How am I to observe myself without a cause? The cause generally is punishment and reward. Which is obviously too absurd, like a dog being trained. So can I look at myself without any motive? Go on, sirs.

IS: At this stage of inquiry, where I am beginning to try to do it, I cannot do it, I am too conditioned.

K: No, I wouldn't admit that. You are always asking for help.

IS: No, but in the same way that I do physical training, I can slowly, but not immediately, be able to look at, to bear, the proximity of those things that normally I do not like to see in myself.

K: I understand that, madam. I have no muscles to do certain exercises, in a week's time I will have those muscles by doing exercises. That same mentality is carried over to "I don't know myself but I will gradually learn about myself."

IS: It is not that I need to gradually learn about myself—we have to be very careful here—it is only that I have to develop the courage, the strength to bear myself.

K: It is the same thing, the same thing. I haven't the strength, physical strength to do certain exercises. The same mental operation goes on psychologically: I am weak, but I must be strong.

IS: It is not that I must get strong. I think this is where one gets oneself into a . . .

K: Cul de sac.

IS: Yes, it is not for the motive, there is very real suffering, and looking at it again and again, and there is a changing factor in this which in the end makes it possible.

K: Which is again gradual evolution. I say that is totally—if I may point out, I am not correcting you—that will lead nowhere, that is totally an illusion.

IS: It need not lead anywhere, but if it is continued in that spirit, with that attitude, not "I get something out of it," then there is a sudden change which is possible, and it does occur. And I would like to make another point here. Whether we have done it starting slowly with that motive, or whether we have done it unbeknownst to ourselves so that it can happen suddenly on the basis of the life that we have lived, does not really make any difference.

K: Madam, either you have insight immediately or you don't have it.

IS: Yes, that is true, but . . .

K: Ah, that means preparation, that means time, which means cultivating, identification, the "me."

IS: No.

K: Of course. The moment you allow time, it is the cultivation of the self.

IS: Not necessarily, sir.

K: Why do you say not necessarily?

IS: If I do it for something that I want to get out of it, then it is certainly a cultivation of the self.

K: Madam, when you say, as we said just now, insight is devoid of time and memory, insight is timeless, it must happen. You can't come to it gradually, it is not a thing cultivated by thought. So to have an insight into oneself instantly, not by degrees. Is that possible?

IS: Yes.

K: No, don't say "Yes," we are inquiring.

IS: Then I would say from my own conviction and experience, "Yes, it is possible."

K: That means if you have an insight, that insight wipes away the self, not just momentarily. So would you say action then is without motive? Do you know such action—not occasionally, but in everyday life? I don't want to be fed occasionally, I want to be fed every day. I don't want to be happy occasionally. So as insight is devoid of time and divorced from memory and thought, is there an action born of insight? You understand?

WR: If you have insight—I don't say "had," because that means memory again—if you have insight, all your actions are without exception free from motive.

K: Again, forgive me—are we talking theoretically or actually?

WR: Actually.

K: That means action is correct, accurate, right through life.

WR: Yes. Technically, you may make mistakes.

K: No, I am not talking of making mistakes technically.

WR: There is no self, there is no motive if you have that insight. Every action . . .

K: Have you got that insight? Not "you," sir—has one that insight into the whole nature of the self? Not arguments, not inductions, not deductions, not conclusions, but has one an insight into the nature of the self? And if there is such an insight into the nature of the self, then action will inevitably follow from that insight.

IS: May I make one point clear that I feel strongly about—it is not that "I" have the insight, that is not possible. There is that insight. It is not as if "I" had it.

K: "I" have no insight. I'm only blind if I say, "'I' have an insight into that." I am a little bit mentally deranged. So what are we talking about? You asked a question, sir.

WR: Of course we have gone very far away from my question.

K: I know. Let's go back to it.

WR: No, you have answered that question. There is another question relating to intelligence. You see there is a theory—perhaps you are aware of this—that we think in a language. Many people say that. Sometimes one is asked, "In which language do you think?" I say I don't know. There is no language in thinking. Thought has no language, and a thought is immediately interpreted into the nearest language.

K: Sir, could you convey your thought to me without the word?

WR: That is the issue. When you convey the thought, it is interpreted.

K: No, sir. Can you convey your thought to me without the word?

WR: That depends on the level of the two people.

K: Which means what?

WR: I don't know whether you accept it, or whether you have that experience, that there is communication without talking, without words.

K: That is, sir, there can only be communication, communion, when you and I are on the same level, and with the same intensity, at the same time. Right? Which is what? When you and I are on the same level, with the same intensity, at the same time, what is that thing? Then words are not necessary.

WR: No.

K: What is that thing?

WR: You can say, if you like, that it is thought.

K: No, sir, when both of us are like that, what is the quality of that state? Not the absence of thought, but the quality, the perfume, the thing of it. Wouldn't you call that love?

WR: Yes.

K: No, don't, don't.

WR: But you asked me. Or are you going to answer? [*laughter*] I get confused when you put a question and I think you expect me to answer!

K: Sir, when two people have the extraordinary quality of this state, words are not necessary. Where that quality of love exists, words become unnecessary. There is instant communication. Now for most of us, language drives us. Language drives us, pushes us, shapes us. Our minds are conditioned by language, by words that drive us, force us. I am an Englishman—the language, and the content of that language. Right? And if we use words without the language directing us, words then have an entirely different meaning.

GN: The language doesn't drive you, but you drive the language.

K: That's right.

DB: I think that ordinarily we are identified with our language and therefore it is driving us, but if we are free of identification . . .

K: That's right, sir, it is extraordinary how language has made us. I am a Communist, I am a Catholic.

DB: That's an identification. Do you think that language is the major source of identification?

K: One of them.

DB: One of the big ones.

K: Yes.

WR: I don't know whether it will be useful, I would like to recall here a very important Mahayana Buddhist philosophical view. It is said that the world is caught up in language—*namakaya, padakaya-vyanjana*—and that the ordinary man is stuck in words like an elephant in mud, and so one must go beyond words—*namapada-vyanjana*—to see them. Because as long as you are, as you say, driven by language . . .

K: Are you?

WR: Are you asking personally?

K: [*laughs*] Yes, are you? Am I? And Dr. Bohm, is he driven by language?

WR: That I can't say. You answer that.

K: I can answer for myself, but I am asking you.

WR:Yes, you answer for yourself.

K: Oh, absolutely.

WR: That's enough. [*laughs*]

K: No, that's not enough!

GN: But I think the more skillful or scholarly one becomes with language, the greater the possibility of being caught in it.

WR: Yes, certainly.

GN: Whereas a rustic might just use it for simple communication.

K: Sir, that was your question, whether thought has words, whether thought is part of words. Does the word create the thought, or thought create the word?

DB: You once asked whether there is a thought without the word.

K: That is very interesting. Shall we go into it a little bit? Do you want to go into it?

WR: Is there a thought without the word?

DB: That is the question.

WR: I think thought has no word, thought is an image.

K: No, we are using word in the sense of symbol, image, picture.

DB: The word can easily be turned into an image, for example, by an artist—a description can be turned by an artist into an image, or vice versa, the image could be described and turned into words. So they have an equivalent content.

K: Sir, what is the origin of thought? If you had to find out—not what the Buddha said, if you, as a human being, had to find out, otherwise your head would be chopped off. It is tremendously important that you must find the origin of thought. What will you do? Please sir, answer that question.

WR: Is there an origin?

K: There must be.

WR: Why?

K: In you, sir, what is the origin of thought?

WR: There is no origin.

K: Of course, sir, there must be a beginning of thought.

WR: That is again a fallacy, a wrong way of looking at it, to assume that everything must have a beginning.

K: No, I am not assuming that everything has a beginning. I am just asking, in order to find out, what is the beginning of thought? How did thought begin? The animals, a dog, everything that is living thinks or feels in various ways. There must be a beginning of that. What is it in human beings?

IS: If we had no desire at all, we would have no thoughts.

K: No, it is not a question of that.

DB: Are you discussing thought without identification?

K: No. How did thought begin in myself? Was it handed down by my father, my parents, by education, by environment, by the past? I want to know. What made me think? Go on, sir. What made you think?

WR: You are putting some cause behind it, but I would say that nothing made me think; thinking is in one's nature. There is no other cause.

K: Oh yes there is. I'll show you.

WR: What is it?

K: No, I am not the final authority. I'd like to talk it over. If I had no memory, would there be thinking?

WR: I ask you again, what is the origin of memory?

K: That's fairly simple to answer. Suppose I remember seeing you in Paris. That is recorded, isn't it? Right, sir?

WR: It is generally accepted that it is recorded in the brain.

K: No, it is an ordinary fact.

WR: No, that I do not accept. It is an old nineteenth-century, eighteenth-century theory that everything is recorded somewhere in the brain.

K: No, sir. Look, I meet you this week, you come back a year later—I hope you will—and then I say, Yes, I recognize you. How does that recognition take place?

WR: This is a question that I very much wanted to ask you.

K: I meet you now, and in a year's time you come back—I hope you will—for a discussion. Then I say, Yes, Mr. Rahula, we met last year. How does that take place? It is very simple. The brain has recorded that memory of meeting you, learning your name. So that is memory, and when I meet you next time I recognize you.

WR: How does it happen?

K: It is very simple. You have been introduced to me, we have sat down here for a morning and two afternoons, and when you come back next year I say, Yes, I remember. If I didn't remember, I wouldn't recognize you. Right? So recording goes on—whether it is the nineteenth, the first, or the twentieth century—recording must go on. The elaborate, educating process of learning a technique, how to drive a car, or go to the moon, whatever it is, is careful accumulation of memory, which then acts. There is nothing wrong in that, is there?

WR: How does it happen?

K: Sir, I don't know how to drive a car, so I go to the man who teaches me how to drive a car. I take twenty-four lessons, at the end of it I am inspected, and the man says, Pretty good. I have learned it by driving with him, he tells me, Be careful, turn to the left, he is guiding me all the time. So at the end of twenty-four lessons I am a good driver, I hope. And that's all. There is nothing right or wrong about it. In the same way I meet you today, and next year I will remember, so there is remembrance, which is the recording process. No? It is so simple.

WR: It is not so completely clear to me. Let us admit it is recorded. How does that record come up when we meet next year?

K: When I see you. That memory springs up and says, Oh, he is Mr. Rahula. And the recording is the image, pleasurable or not pleasurable.

WR: I hope it will be pleasurable! [*laughter*]

K: And that is recorded, and when I meet you next time, I meet you. But if it is not pleasurable I say, Oh, what a bore. And I turn away and talk about something else. So this whole process is recording—how I learned to drive a car, how I learned to speak English, French, German, whatever it is, there must be recording. No?

WR: Certainly it is so.

K: But you said this was a nineteenth-century view.

WR: What I want to say is that it is not in the brain. That is the thing. It is in the nature of what we generally call the mental faculty. Just as I hear noise and so on by its particular faculty, there is also the mental faculty. Recording is one of its potentialities.

K: It is the faculty of the brain to record.

WR: My point is that it is not the physical brain.

K: Ah, you have gone off into something!

WR: Yes, that is what I say.

GN: Are you saying that the mental faculty is spread all over the body, not necessarily in the head?

K: Oh no.

WR: Our mental faculty is one of the sense organs—there are five physical sense organs. The eye has the power to see and examine; the ear can't do it, it can only hear. There is the mental faculty, just as there are the physical faculties—the eye, ear, nose, tongue, the body—that deal with the external, the material world. But that is only part of the world; the bigger part of the world is not touched by that.

K: What is the bigger part of the world?

WR: All the sensations that we were talking about, all these things are not touched by the body, or anything like that. There it is the mind, the mental faculty, which has many aspects, many potentialities, one of which is memory. And what I want you to clarify is: How does it happen? And of course you begin with the idea that it is the brain, which is recording, which I dispute.

K: Sir, let's cut out the brain for the moment. I meet you today and I see you a week later. There is the process of recognition. All right, that's one part of the faculty. The other part of the faculty is to think logically, or not logically. So there are several aspects, faculties, which make up the mind. You cannot have mind without the brain.

WR: Yes, not only the brain, you can't have a mind without the body, the stomach, the heart, without physical existence.

K: That's all. Therefore mind is part of the senses, mind is part of thought, emotions, certain faculties, and so on and so on. Is that outside, or is the whole structure of the organism, the whole brain, body, eyes, ears, all that, part of this mind which is the process of thinking?

DB: Are you saying mind is thought, or is it more than thought as well?

K: I don't know, but I don't want to say that. I only want to say that the mind, as long as it is functioning within the field of thought, is limited.

DB: You mean consciousness, the mind, is that.

K: Yes, consciousness is limited.

DB: We are saying it is limited by these faculties, wherever they are.

K: Yes, that's right, whatever they are.

DB: But as far as recognition goes, people are even making machines that can imitate the process of recognition.

K: Of course.

DB: Simple things can already be recognized by computers.

IS: And yet, if I have met you just for a moment, and the image of that meeting does not have a sufficient impact on me, I will next week pass you by and not recognize you.

DB: That's the point, it has to be recorded with some energy.

K: All recording must have energy.

DB: If you don't turn the microphone on, nothing is recorded.

WR: And many things that we see and hear we don't remember, only things that leave a certain impression.

DB: You see, I think it is fairly clear how the record could give rise to a recognition from the next experience. The next time you see the person the record is compared with him.

WR: It comes back.

DB: Yes.

WR: It is exactly like the computer.

K: So our brains are computers.

WR: I should say, no, not the brain.

K: What is the brain?

WR: The brain may be the basis—but why do you only say the brain? Can you think without the whole body, without the heart?

K: No, sir, we have said that. The mind contains the brain, the feelings, the heart, the whole structure.

DB: All the nerve centers.

K: We are using the word "mind" as consciousness, and I cannot have consciousness if the heart doesn't function.

WR: That is why I used the word "mental faculty" instead of "mind" or "consciousness," the word "faculty" embracing and involving all those functions.

K: What do you mean by the word "faculty"? What does the word mean, sir?

DB: To have some capacity and ability, the capacity to do something.

WR: The ability to do, as in the case of the visual faculty.

K: No, sir, the ability to do depends on knowledge. If I didn't know how to play the piano, if I have not learned it . . .

WR: No, excuse me, sir, you are going away from the point. I said the mental faculty—mind—has the power, the capacity, the potentiality, to do all that. And those are different aspects of the thing.

K: Oh, I see.

DB: The faculty is inborn.

WR: Inborn, innate, in itself has the power. And you can't ask why and from where.

K: No, I won't ask that. But I won't accept the mind has the inborn faculty . . .

DB: To think.

K: Inborn, which means it is not genetic, it is not heredity.

DB: No, "inborn" means genetic.

WR: Let us say the mind, just like our eyes, has the power to see.

K: So the mind has the power . . .

WR: . . . to do all those tricks, all those things that we are talking about—the memory, reaction, sensation, and all that.

K: The mind is the active energy to do all that.

DB: Well, also the physical structure is all over the body. I think it is a good analogy to say that the eye has certain possibilities, and in its body the infant has the ability to think already built into him because of heredity.

K: How has this "built in" come into being?

DB: By growing in the same way that the eye grew. You see, the eye has a tremendous . . .

K: Which means evolution.

DB: Evolution, yes.

K: Wait, go slowly. Which means right from the beginning it has evolved until we are now monkeys, greater monkeys. Sorry!

WR: Again I question that. You have taken Darwin's theory for granted, that we evolve from the monkeys.

K: I don't take Darwin for granted, I see this happening in the world.

WR: When you say we have evolved from the monkey . . .

K: We have evolved from imperfect man; or have not evolved from perfect man. We are going downhill instead of uphill, or we are going uphill, therefore we are imperfect man.

DB: I wonder if we want to discuss all these things, they are really details that are not certain.

WR: That is why I object to the statement about evolving from the monkey. We don't know.

K: I don't know, sir, I don't know how we have evolved, but I do know the very simple thing that without recording there is no thought.

WR: That means that thought is memory.

K: Of course. Thought is memory, which is experience, which is knowledge, stored up—it doesn't matter where, in my big toe—and when it is challenged, it operates.

DB: Well, we have also said thought is the ability to reason logically and along with the memory, all that together.

K: Think logically, or illogically, and so on.

DB: All of what you have called faculties.

WR: Yes, I used that word because it covers a bigger field.

DB: But you are saying it still depends on memory.

K: Of course, a sense of recording is memory.

DB: Without memory none of the other faculties could operate.

K: Of course not. I see that thing, it has been called a tree, I call it a tree. That's all. There is recording all the time, without that recording there is no beginning of thought, there is no thought. Sir, if you were born in the Catholic world, and conditioned by the Catholic world, you would be thinking according to the Catholic world, to Christ, you know, to the whole business of it. So you are conditioned by propaganda, by books, by priests, by all the circus that goes on, as you are conditioned in India, or Ceylon, and so on. So what is the origin, the beginning of this conditioning? Why does man condition himself? For security, to avoid danger? Obviously. I believe in Christ, because I have been brought up in the Christian world, that is my conditioning, and this life is a miserable, unhappy life, but I believe in Christ, which gives me a certain sense of comfort, of strength to face this appalling thing, the world. So it gives me great comfort. That's all. It gives me security in an insecure world, psychologically, the Father is looking after me. And the Hindus, the Buddhists, the Muslims, they are all in the same category. So the instinctual response of a human being is to feel secure, like a child, obviously. No?

WR: How does it come about, that sense of security, the feeling of security, what is the origin of that?

K: The mother and the child, the baby, they must have a little security, the baby must have security, physical security, it must have food at the right times, at the right hour, and all the rest of it.

DB: Does the baby have a feeling of security at the same time?

K: Probably, I don't know, not being a baby, and not remembering, but I am sure that it feels safe.

DB: It feels safe.

K: Safe, looked after, quiet, the moment it cries the mother is there, to change the diapers, to feed it and all the rest of it. What's

89

wrong with that? From that physical security we turn to psychological security, which Christ gives me. It may be nonsense, unreasonable and all kinds of things, but I like that, at least I have comfort in some illusion. But I don't call it illusion. If *you* call it illusion, I will kick you. So we go on that way. You have your security in something, I have my security, and another has his security in Islam, and so on. So each one of us clings to our own particular form of security, whether it is reasonable, sane, rational, that doesn't matter.

DB: It seems to me that it is similar to the pleasure question; that is you register the feeling of pleasure and then try to build it up.

K: I can't say, Well, I'll let go of Christ. I say, My God, I can't.

DB: It is the same with pleasure, you can't give up pleasure.

K: Of course, the same problem.

IS: I think it is harder with pleasure, because people nowadays do seem as if they give up or change their religions without too much difficulty, but when it really comes to it we are all much against giving up our pleasure.

K: Ah well, physical pleasure, that's a different matter altogether.

IS: Or pleasures of the mind.

K: Of course.

WR: But where are we going?

K: Where are we going? I haven't finished yet. We haven't discussed the central issue of life: what is action without this enormous complex of motives, reactions, regrets, pain, sorrow? Can a human live in action without all this dreadful confusion? That's all. And you say, Yes, you can so live. And you tell me, if you are a Christian, Believe in God, believe in Christ, he will save you from all this. And I am so unhappy, I say, For God's sake, and I cling to it. And if you are X, you say, I believe in all the things the Buddha has said—*Buddham saranam gachchami*—that is good enough for me. I will take comfort in that. So my actions are based on reward and punishment. Right, sir? If I do this I will reach nirvana, if I don't I'll go to hell, which is the Christian idea and all the rest of it. Being fairly intelligent and educated, one has thrown all that overboard, one says all that is nonsense. I want to find out if there is an action without any shadow of effort and regret. You understand, sir? It is important to find out, not theoretically or casually, it is a burning question for me, a passionate thing. I must find out because I don't want to enter the cage, the rat race. So what shall I do? What is right action under all circumstances, which doesn't depend on circumstances? My wife says, Do this, I love you but you must do this, or something else. I put away all those influences or pressures, but I want to find out if there is an action which is complete in itself.

So I must understand if there is an action that is total, which is complete, whole, not partial. Which means can I observe myself wholly, not in fragments? Or through the fragment instantly see the whole? So is there an action that is whole? I say, yes, there is, definitely. Don't you ask me what it is?

WR: I wanted to ask but I was waiting for the answer.

K: Ask it!

WR: I want to ask you. What is that?

K: First of all, can you see with your eyes the tree as a whole? Can you see your wife or husband, or girlfriend or boyfriend, as a whole entity? Do you understand my question? Can you see anything totally, or are you always seeing partially?

WR: When you use the word "totally," what is its meaning?

K: Whole. Don't go to something else. Can I see you as a whole being? You understand? Can I see humanity as myself, which is the whole? That's good enough. Can I see humanity as myself? Because humanity is like me, suffering, miserable, confused, in agony, terrified, insecure, sorrow-ridden, like another. Right? So in seeing man, humanity, I see myself.

WR: Or the other way round. By seeing yourself you see humanity.

K: Which is me. It doesn't matter whether you say, I see myself as humanity, then humanity is me. I am not separate from humanity, I don't say, I am part of an elite. I am this, I am like the rest of the gang. So I see the world as myself, which is the whole. That's simple, sir—not simple, it *is*—would that be right, sir?

DB: I was wondering if, as you said, we could consider the tree for a moment.

K: The tree is too petty.

DB: It is not clear when you say you see the tree as a whole . . .

K: The whole thing, to see something wholly, sir.

DB: Just see it all, right.

IS: I think we are in a slight language difficulty because we have no other possibilities. This "I see as a whole" really means that the self, or the fallacy of the self, has clearly been seen into, and has broken down, because otherwise however much I see the tree as a whole, it is still my thought.

K: That is the ultimate thing. But can you see your husband, your wife, or your girlfriend, as a whole being? Totally, you know. You can, can't you? How does that happen when you can see somebody wholly?

IS: Tremendous warmth—but not mine.

K: No.

IS: Warmth comes into it.

K: If you love that tree, you will see it wholly.

IS: But we have also to be careful what we mean by love.

K: Keep it very simple, don't intellectualize it for the moment, we'll do it later. If I love somebody, love not possessively, acquisitively, all the rest of that nonsense, if I love, the whole thing is there, the totality of that man or woman is there. So can I see myself wholly, myself being humanity? I am not different from humanity. I am not an individual. That's all phony. I am the rest of the world, I am the world. Can I see that as a whole? I am not a Communist, sir, because the Communists say that too, but I am not that—stupid Communists.

WR: Why do you want to deny Communism like that? What is wrong if you are a Communist?

K: You have misunderstood my point. Communists are full of theories and putting those theories into practice and shaping man according to a theory. Leave that aside; I am sorry I brought that up. To look at myself, I can see myself as a whole only when I am actually the rest of mankind.

DB: You mean in essence, you mean that essentially I am the same as the whole.

K: Essentially, basically.

DB: The basic qualities.

K: I may have a long nose, or short nose, and crooked eyes, or blue eyes, but I am not talking about that.

IS: A human being.

K: As a human being. Then there is no individual effort, nor collective effort. Right? When one sees oneself as a whole, the parts disappear. But we think by collecting the parts we make the whole. So when I see myself as a whole, then the parts disappear, therefore the self is not. Sir, when I see that thing, that tree, completely, I can see it completely only if I don't condemn and if I don't say, "It's my tree, it's my garden." Right? You understand what I am saying?

WR: Yes.

K: So when I love that tree, I see it as a whole.

DB: Would you also say then that it is similar to all trees? Like saying, if I see myself as a whole, I am the same as all mankind.

K: So I love all trees.

DB: Is that the same?

K: Of course, obviously.

DB: It doesn't depend on that single tree. It is not just *this* tree that you love.

K: It isn't that elm that I love.

DB: That is right here in this place.

K: I love the trees, whether they are in your garden, or my garden, or somewhere else, in a field.

DB: Wherever it is. So the particulars don't matter.

K: That's it.

IS: I love the tree and see it whole because I love it. It doesn't mean that all trees are the same, the *love* is the same.

K: I raised the question of seeing wholly because of the question: What is action which is not fragmented, not broken up as a businessman, an artist, a lecturer, a professor, a priest, an action which is total? Don't say, If the self is not, then you will have it. But I have a self, one is caught in the self; or rather the self is there.

DB: But you are suggesting, see the self whole and then it will change and not be there.

K: Yes, sir.

DB: Therefore would you also say that you have to love the self?

K: That is a dangerous statement. I was going to make it, and I stopped myself in time [*laughs*] because that is what advertising people say: Reward yourself, love your hair, use this shampoo.

DB: Could you say instead: You are mankind, you love mankind?

K: Ah, now, be careful.

DB: Because the analogy seems to be limited.

K: Analogies are limited.

IS: So are the words in themselves.

K: Any more questions, sir? We will stop unless you have more.

WR: There is no end to these questions, therefore let us finish today like that. But you have answered all my questions, and thank you very much for all your very enlightening explanations.

What Is Truth?

Fourth Conversation with the Buddhist Scholar
Walpola Rahula, and with Professor David Bohm
and Others

WALPOLA RAHULA: I want to ask you one thing. We all talk of truth, absolute truth, ultimate truth; and seeing it and realizing it; we always talk about it. According to Buddha's teaching, these are very important central points, the essence really. And Buddha says clearly that there is only one truth, there is no second—*ekam hi saccam na dutiyam atthi*. But this is never defined in positive terms. This truth is also equated with nirvana. The terms ultimate or absolute truth are used as synonyms of nirvana.

Nirvana is never defined, except in mostly negative terms. If it is described in positive terms, it is mostly metaphorically, in a symbolic way. And as you know, there was the original, authentic teaching of the Buddha called the Theravada, the "tradition of the elders." Then about the first century B.C., the Mahayana, a later development, began to grow, as a free interpretation of the Buddha's teaching. And there is a very beautiful Mahayana text called the *Vimalakirtinirdesha-sutra*, the teaching of the bodhisattva Vimalakirti. At a great gathering of bodhisattvas and disciples in his house, the question was put: "What is nonduality?" That is, "nonduality" is another word for the absolute truth or nirvana. In Sanskrit it is called *advaya*.

KRISHNAMURTI: *Advaita*, in Sanskrit, yes.

WR: No, *advaita* is different from *advaya*. The Vedanta *advaita* means "You are the world, there is no difference." In Buddhist terminology, *advaya* means "neither existence nor nonexistence." The Buddha says that the conventional world is duality, that means, either is or is not, either exists or does not exist, either is right or wrong, that is *dvaya*, according to Buddhist teaching. According to the Buddha, the world depends on *dvaya*. But the Buddha teaches without falling into this error. The question was "What is *advaya*?" And there are thirty-two definitions given by various bodhisattvas and disciples. So the assembly asks Vimalakirti for his opinion. And the sutra says—it is very interesting—that Vimalakirti answered the question with a thundering silence.

K: Quite.

WR: If you speak, it is not nonduality. When I gave a series of lectures in Oxford, a professor asked me: "Can you formulate this nonduality or truth?" I said the moment you formulate it, that is not nonduality; it becomes duality the moment you formulate it. So, just as they asked Vimalakirti long ago, I ask you today: What is truth, what is absolute truth, what is ultimate truth, and what is that nonduality as you see it? Tell us. It is a challenge.

K: Do you think, sir, there is a difference between reality and truth? And is truth measurable by words? If we could distinguish between what is reality and what is truth, then perhaps we could penetrate more deeply into this question. What is reality? The word *res* means "thing." What is the thing? Could we say that everything that thought has created is reality—including the illusions, the gods, the various mantras, the rituals, the whole movement of thought, what it has brought about in the world, the cathedrals, the temples, the mosques, and their content? That is reality. Like the microphone—it is made by thought, it is there, actual. But nature is not created by thought. It exists. The beauty of the Earth, the rivers, the seas, the heavens, the stars, the flowing winds. But we human beings have used nature to produce things, like our houses, chairs, and so on. I mean, a beautiful cathedral, a beautiful poem, a lovely picture, are all the result of thought. So could we say then that anything that thought has created, brought about, put together, is reality?

MARY ZIMBALIST: When you speak of the beauty of the object, are you including that quality of beauty as reality, or the object itself, with beauty perhaps being some other quality? Are you including the idea of the beauty of that object in this category?

K: The object itself could be beautiful, or one can attribute beauty to an object that may not be beautiful in itself. So could we say, sir, that everything that thought has put together, including the illusions it has created, and the material things it has created through technological knowledge and so on, could we say that all that is reality?

WR: Yes. May I add a little to that? According to Buddhist thought, Buddha's teaching, there is relative truth or reality.

K: Don't let's use "truth" and "reality" just yet.

WR: Yes, let us say reality. Reality is relative and absolute.

K: Of course.

WR: What you say is fully accepted, that is reality.

K: That is, everything that thought has created is reality. Dreams, all the sensory and sensuous responses, the whole techno-

logical world, all the things that thought has put together as literature, poems, paintings, illusions, gods, symbols—all that is reality.
Would you accept that?

PHIROZ MEHTA: Yes, but the word "reality" has its denotation,
its first meaning as well as its connotations. And through the centuries people have tended to talk of reality more in terms of one of
its connotations of ultimate reality.

K: I know, but I would like to separate the two—truth and
reality. Otherwise we mix up our terms all the time.

PM: That is true.

SCOTT FORBES: Are you also including nature in reality?

K: No, that tree is not created by thought. But out of that tree
man can produce chairs and so on.

SF: Is there, then, a third category of things, which is neither
truth nor reality? Or are you calling nature . . .

K: Nature is not created by thought. The tiger, the elephant,
the deer, the gazelle—they are obviously not created by thought.

WR: That means you don't take a tree as a reality.

K: I take it as a reality, of course it's a reality, but it's not created
by thought.

WR: That's true. Then are you saying that you include only
things created by thought in reality?

K: Yes.

WR: Of course, that is your own definition.

K: No, I'm trying to be clear about our understanding of the
two terms "truth" and "reality."

WR: Yes, I understand, leave the word "truth" for another
purpose.

K: Not another purpose. Let us look at reality—what is reality? The world is reality.

WR: Yes.

K: These lamps are reality. You sitting there, this person sitting here, are realities. The illusions that one has are an actual reality.

MZ: But sir, the people sitting there are not created by thought.

K: No.

MZ: So could we more or less define another category for living creatures, nature, trees, animals, and people?

K: A human being is not created by thought. But what he creates is.

MZ: Yes. So the reality category of which you are speaking is man-made, in a sense.

K: Man-made. Like war is a reality. You're a bit hesitant about this.

PM: Could we regard all that is apprehended through the senses, and then interpreted by the brain, as reality?

K: That's right, sir.

SF: At one time we made a distinction, when talking, between reality, which was anything that was created by the mind, and actuality, which is anything that could be captured by the mind, anything that exists in time and space.

K: Yes.

SF: And then there is truth. Now, reality was part of actuality. In other words, the tree was an actuality, not a reality.

K: Why do you want to separate?

SF: Otherwise it becomes very confusing, because if we say, Look, you and I, as people, are not created by thought, we are not reality.

K: You want to separate actuality, reality, and truth. Is that it?

SF: Well, I just offer that as a convenient definition of words that we used before.

K: Would we say that the actual is what is happening now?

PM: Yes, that's a good way of putting it. The point that arises there is: Are we capable of apprehending the totality of what is happening now? We apprehend only a portion of it.

K: Yes, but that is a different point, we can go into that. But what is happening is actual. That's all. Not whether we understand, comprehend the whole of it or part of it and so on. What is happening is the actual.

PM: Yes, that is the fact.

K: That is a fact. So what do you say to all this, sirs?

WR: I am still hesitating, I'm waiting to see more.

K: Whether a mind can see the actual incompletely or completely, that's not the point for the moment. The question is whether the mind can apprehend, perceive, observe, or see that from reality you cannot get to truth.

STEPHEN SMITH: That's quite a big jump, probably.

K: Sir, could we put it this way too: as you pointed out, all the sensory responses are the beginning of thought. And thought, with all its complex movements, is what is happening now when we are talking. And what is happening is the actual, and the interpretation or the understanding of what is happening depends on thought. All that, including illusion and the whole business of it, is reality.

PM: Yes, that is so.

K: If we agree or accept that for the moment, then the question arises: Can the mind, which is the network of all the senses, actualities and so on, apprehend, see, observe what is truth?

PM: Provided the mind can be free of all its conditioning.

K: I'll come to that a little later. But that is the problem. To find out what absolute truth is, thought must be understood—the whole movement and the nature of thought must be gone into, observed—and so has its relative place. And the mind therefore becomes absolutely still; and perhaps, in that stillness, truth is perceived, which is not to be measured by words.

PM: Yes, there I'd agree completely.

WR: Yes, I agree with that.

K: Now, there are these two. A human being is caught in the movement of thought. And this movement projects what truth is.

PM: This is the mistake that man makes.

K: Of course, he projects from this to that, hoping to find what truth is. Or projects what he thinks is truth. And the truth can be put in different words—God, Brahman, as it is called in India, or nirvana or *moksha*, all that business. So our next question is: Can the mind cease to measure?

PM: That is to say, the mind as it functions at present in each one of us as an individual.

K: As human beings. Measurement is our whole educational, environmental, and social conditioning. Would you agree?

WR: Yes.

K: Then what is measurement?

PM: Limitation.

K: No, what is measurement, to measure? I measure a piece of cloth, or measure the height of the house, measure the distance from here to a certain place, and so on. Measurement means comparison.

SS: Well, there is also psychological measurement in all this.

K: Yes, there is physical measurement and psychological measurement. One measures oneself psychologically against somebody. And so there is this constant measurement of comparison, both externally and inwardly. But I'm giving a lecture—what's the idea?

WR: Well, I put the question to you that they put to Vimalakirti.

K: What is the question?

WR: What is nonduality, what is truth?

K: As long as thought is measuring there must be duality. Now, how has this conditioning come about? You understand, sir? Otherwise we can't move away from this to that. How has this constant measurement, comparison, imitation—you know, the whole movement of measurement, why has man been caught in it?

WR: All measurement is based on self.

K: Yes, but how has it come about? Why are human beings, wherever they live, conditioned through this measurement? One wants to find out the source of this measurement.

SS: Part of it seems to be the fruit of observation, because you observe the duality of life in terms of night and day, man and woman, the change of seasons, and this kind of thing, there is a certain kind of contrast, a certain apparent contrast. So it may seem a natural step to say that there is therefore a kind of contrast or comparison that is applicable to human life.

K: There is darkness and light, thunder and silence.

PARCHURE: It seems that thought needs a static point to measure, and as it is itself in a constant state of flux or movement, it cannot measure, so it creates a static point that is immovable, which is taken as the center of the self. And from there only can it measure.

K: Yes, I mean, the very words "better" and "greater" in the

English language are measurement. So the language itself is involved in measurement. Now, one needs to find out, doesn't one, what the source of this measurement is, why the human being has employed this as a means of living? One sees night and day, a high mountain and low valleys, a tall man, a short man, a woman, a man, a child, old age—physically there are all these states of measurement. There is also psychological measurement, that is what I'm talking about, much more than the mere physical movement of distance and so on. Why has man been held in this measurement?

SS: Probably he thinks it is the way forward to some extent, because if you're a farmer and you plant a crop in a certain way, and you get a poor result, the next year you plant in a different way, and you get a better result.

K: Yes, so it is time. Go on, sir, a bit more.

SS: It includes the ability to reflect, to have experience, to reflect on experience, to produce something better out of that experience in terms of, probably, an established notion of what is the good, what is the better thing to have, or what is the right situation of things.

K: Of course, but I want to go a little further than that. Why has man used time as a means of progress? I'm talking psychologically, not of time that is necessary to learn a language, to develop a certain technology, and so on.

P: Perhaps the need for security of thought for itself.

K: No, time, which is measurement.

PM: Do you think that our tendency is that starting with the physical facts of difference in size, in quantity, and so forth, we apply that analogically to the psychological process?

K: Yes, that's what I want to get at. Without measurement, there would have been no technology.

PM: That's true.

GIDDU NARAYAN: In science and mathematics, as they advance, measurement becomes more and more refined, and each refinement leads to a further step of progress, in computers and so on. So in that area, in science and technology, measurement and refinement of measurement do lead to a certain kind of progress.

K: Of course, we are not denying that.

WR: But we are not talking of physical measurement so much as psychological measurement.

K: Yes. Why has man used psychological time as a means of self-growth, self-aggrandizement? He calls it getting "better," getting more noble, achieving enlightenment. All that implies time.

GN: Is it, as Mehta says, carried over from the day-to-day living of physical measurement to the psychological field? Is it carried over, or does it exist in the psychological field without reference to this?

K: That's what we are discussing. Whether there is any psychological evolution at all.

SF: Could we say that we began to apply measurement to the psychological field out of habit, because that is what we have been using for the physical field, but also could we have made that transfer because it's very comfortable to think that I might be in a mess now but later on I'll be fine?

K: Of course, sir. Let's be clear on this. At the technological, physical level, we need time. We need time to acquire a language, time to build a house, time to go from here to there or for developing a technology or science; we need time there. So let's be clear on that. But I'm asking something else. Do we need time at all, psychologically?

SHAKUNTALA NARAYAN: What is it that creates time?

K: Thought, thought is time.

SN: So doesn't thought have something to do with it?

K: Which is what we are saying: time is movement. So thought is movement, time is movement from here to there; one is greedy, envious, I need time to be free of it. Physical distance and psychological distance. One is questioning whether that is not an illusion—not the physical distance, but the psychological distance. To put it very succinctly, is there, psychologically, tomorrow?

PM: Only in terms of anticipation.

K: Ah, because thought says, I hope to . . .

PM: And in addition to thought, there is the fact of our physical experience, of day and night, and therefore the words "tomorrow" and "today."

K: There is yesterday, today, and tomorrow; that is a reality, that is also a measurement. But we are asking: Is there psychological time at all, or has thought invented time, psychological time, in order to feel that it can achieve or live in some kind of security?

WR: What is time?

K: Time, sir, is movement.

WR: Yes, time is nothing but the unbroken continuity of cause and effect. That is movement.

K: Movement, we said. Cause, effect, effect becomes the cause, and so on.

WR: That is time. We give the word "time" to that movement.

K: Yes, which is movement. It's now five minutes past twelve, it is a movement till it reaches one o'clock. That is one aspect of time. And also the aspect of time that is from here—physical distance. I have to go to London, and it takes time to get there.

WR: Yes, that is another conception of time.

K: Another time. We are looking at the various facets of time.

MZ: Sir, would you say that thought in itself implies time, because the action of the mind in consulting thought, going through the thought process takes time, even if it is a very quick, short amount of time?

K: Surely, because thought is the response of memory, and memory is time. Let's stick to one thing; which is, there is physical time, yesterday, today, and tomorrow, time as movement.

PM: What we call chronological time.

K: Let's call that chronological time. Time also for distance, time also for cause and effect—acorn and tree. To climb a mountain requires time. So we are saying time, physically, exists. Physically, the baby grows into the man and so on. So time is necessary, time exists. That is an actuality, that is a reality. We are questioning whether *psychologically* there is time at all. Or thought has invented time as a means of either achieving security or it is too lazy to completely transform itself, so it says, "Give me time, give me time to be strong psychologically. Psychologically give me time so that I get rid of my anger, my jealousy, or whatever it is, and I'll be free of it." So time is being used as a means of achieving something psychologically.

MZ: But then one must ask you about the use of the word "psychological" in this instance, because if a thought process is involved, and we have just said time is implicit in thought, how can you be without thought psychologically?

K: We are coming to that.

MZ: Or is the psychological realm in this discussion outside of thought, part of thought, or could it be either?

K: Isn't the whole psyche put together by thought?

SS: That seems to be the question here, whether it is or not.

K: I'm asking, sir, go slowly. Isn't the whole psyche the "me"?

SS: Is that the psyche?

K: Isn't it? The "me" is what I think, what I want, what I don't want, and so on. The whole self-centered movement of the "me" is put together by thought.

MZ: If that is so, then how would it be possible for time not to be involved in any psychological movement?

K: We're going to go into that. I want first to be clear that our questions are understood.

GN: Would you make a distinction, sir, between hope and aspiration, because many people say to aspire is something noble, but to hope is . . .

K: Aspiring is time. Hoping is also time.

GN: But in aspiration there seems to be the idea of something very right.

K: I aspire to become God—it's so silly.

GN: Wouldn't you say that there is aspiration in the whole religious endeavor?

WR: Of course, in religious tradition there is always aspiration. What we are discussing, I think, is whether you can see truth without thinking or time, whether seeing truth is *now*, this moment, or whether you postpone it till you become better.

K: Ah, no.

WR: That is the question.

K: That is, the moment you introduce the word "better" . . .

WR: That is what I am saying. Truth is something you see *now*.

K: No, we haven't come to truth yet. I am very careful, sir; I don't want to enter the world of truth yet. One wants to be clear whether one's thinking is logical, sane, and rational, or comes to a conclusion that is illusory. So one wants to examine the whole nature of time, psychologically. That's all I'm talking about. If there is no tomorrow psychologically, our whole action is different. But psychologically, we say, tomorrow is important. Tomorrow I will do this, tomorrow I hope to change, psychologically. I'm questioning that, because all our aspirations, hope, everything, are based on the future, which is time.

GN: You would say, then, that any aspiration, however noble, is in the field of reality?

K: Yes, in the field of thought.

PM: Yes, because it is a formulation.

K: A formulation by thought.

PM: Exactly. So would I be right in saying you are concerned with being totally free of the time factor in psychological terms?

K: Yes, sir. Otherwise I am caught, our mind is living always in a circle.

PM: Yes, that is true. We are tied to the past, to that which has become fossilized.

K: Yes, the past modifying the present and going off into the future. This past modifying itself into the future is time. So when one says, "I will be better, I will understand, or I will try," all these are involved in time. So I question that, whether it's merely an invention of thought for its own purpose— for whatever reason— and so it is illusory and so there is no tomorrow.

PM: In psychological terms.

K: Of course, we said that very clearly. If one is envious, envy is a sensory response, and therefore thought has created this envy. Now generally, we say, Give me time to be free of that envy.

PM: Yes, provided we perceive that this is envy.

K: Oh yes, I'm envious: you've a bigger house, you're better dressed, you've more money, all the rest of it, everybody perceives this envy, this jealousy, this antagonism. So is it possible, being envious, to be free of it instantly and not allow time to intervene? That is the whole point.

PM: Isn't the envy a psychical reaction to what is perceived through the senses?

K: Yes, that's right.

PM: And are not the sense functionings . . .

K: Actual.

PM: Yes, they are. And determined by actual physical conditions?

K: Yes, obviously.

PM: So the psychical reaction follows the sensuous activity, and that involves the pleasure/pain drives within us.

K: Obviously. One sees you driving in a big car, and I'm driving a small car, so there is comparison.

PM: Yes, the comparison arises, surely, partially through what others have put before us, saying that this is better than that, this is more pleasant or this is less pleasant. So we get into the psychological habit.

K: That begins from childhood. You are not as good as your brother in examinations, and the whole education system is based on this comparative evaluation of one's capacities. Now we're going off, you see, we are moving away from . . .

WR: Yes.

SF: Yes, didn't we just come to the fact that anything that is involved in measurement and thought cannot get rid of measurement and thought?

K: First it must realize the actuality of it. Not just say, "Yes, I've understood intellectually."

SF: Does it realize that with thought?

K: No.

SF: So then what is the . . .

K: Wait, we are coming to that slowly. Do we see that we have used time psychologically, and that psychological usage of time is an illusion? First I want to see, we must be clear on that point. I will reach heaven, I will become enlightened, I will eventually, through various series of lives, or one life, achieve nirvana, *moksha*, all that. All that is psychological time. We are questioning whether that thing is an illusion. If it is an illusion, it is a part of thought.

SF: Right. Now we can't, we don't use thought in order to see all this.

K: No, wait. Do we understand even verbally?

SF: Even with thought?

K: With thought. Communication between us now is through words. Those words have been accumulated and so on, and for the moment we both of us speak in English, we understand the meaning. Now, do we see—see not through argument, through explanation, through rationalization—that thought has created this psychological time as a means of achieving something?

MZ: Can we see that still within the thought process, still within the realm of thought?

K: Now, wait.

MZ: Is that the seeing you're talking about?

K: No, I am coming to that. I am coming to that slowly, I want to lead up to it, otherwise it won't be clear. Am I all right, are we following each other or not?

WR: I am following.

K: Is this accurate, sir?

WR: That I can't yet say, because I don't know where we are going.

K: I don't know where I'm going either! [*laughter*] But this is a fact.

WR: Yes, that's right. That is, I am watching.

GN: I think there's also some difficulty in apprehending what you're saying, because there is maturity and growth in nature through time.

K: We've been through that, Narayan, don't go back to it.

GN: I'm not going back to it, but unconsciously you're identified with it. Is there maturity and growth in human beings through time? There is some kind of maturity through time.

K: We said that.

GN: Yes, so one gets stuck to that.

K: One holds on, is attached to this idea of time as self-improvement, not only physically but psychologically.

GN: I don't even say self-improvement, but maturity. Like a kind of natural growth, comparing yourself with nature, as you see everywhere.

K: Yes, but wait, what do you mean by maturity? We may have different meanings for that word "mature." A tree is mature at a certain age. A human being is physically mature at a certain age. And there is mature cheese. [*laughs*]

GN: Yes, the whole, the fruit from the bud.

K: Yes, the fruit is mature to be picked. And so on. But is there psychological maturity at all? That's my whole point.

P: Perhaps there is a factor of life, intellectual maturity, which is at the mental level.

MZ: Within the illusory world, there is a certain maturity psychologically, but it's still founded on thought and time.

K: Yes, but I'm just asking, Maria, do we understand clearly, even verbally and so intellectually, that we have used time as a psychological catalyst to bring about change? And I'm questioning that catalyst.

PM: May I inquire, sir, what precisely you mean by the word "see" when you say, "Do we see that psychological time is an illusion?"

K: I mean by the word "see" to observe without the interference of thought.

PM: That means, to be completely conscious, to be completely aware of the fact that time is an illusion.

K: Yes, to see this as I see a snake, and not mistake it for a rope.

PM: Would you agree that this involves a complete transformation of your mode of awareness, of your consciousness? When you're really conscious of something, you don't have to . . .

K: Now, wait a minute. Again, sir, the words "consciousness" and "conscious" . . .

PM: Those are difficult words.

K: Those are difficult words. I see this—can I see this and not call it a microphone? Not call it anything, but see the shape, just observe without any reflection?

PM: Quite, without naming it.

K: Naming, analyzing, and all the rest of it.

PM: In other words, to see is a whole seeing, almost in the sense of your being what you see.

K: No, then that becomes a duality, you become that.

PM: You don't become that in the sense that you are merged into it. But you are awake in terms of a unitary whole.

K: Just a minute, sir. Those again are rather difficult words.

WR: I don't think that is what he means.

K: Sir, to observe implies—first, let's look at this as it is gener-ally understood—to observe a tree, I name it. I like it or don't like it, and so on. But what we mean by observation, by seeing, is to listen first, and not to make an abstraction of it into an idea so that the idea sees. I wonder if you see this?

WR: Yes, yes.

K: Say, for instance, I said a little earlier that psychologically there is no time, that psychological time is the invention of thought, and may be an illusion. Now to listen to that without interpreting it, thinking, "What do you mean?" rationalizing it, or saying, "I don't understand" or "I do understand," just to listen to that statement and not make an idea of it, but just to listen. And as one listens in that way, in the same way to observe, to see. What do you say, sir?

WR: I want to ask you, what are you trying to tell us?

K: I'm trying to say, sir, that truth cannot possibly be perceived, be seen, through time.

WR: Right.

K: Wait a minute, you can't agree.

WR: Not agree, I see it. That is why I was waiting to ask you what you are trying to say.

K: I'm trying to say that—I'm not trying, I'm saying! [*laughter*]

WR: Yes, of course, what you want to say.

K: Sorry! I'm saying that man, through comparison with the outer world, has created a psychological time as a means of achiev-ing a desired, rewarding end.

WR: I agree.

K: No, do you see that as a fact—a fact in the sense that it is so?

SF: Is the faculty of the mind which sees that the same faculty that sees truth?

K: Look, Scott, first you listen, don't you, to that statement?

SF: Yes.

K: How do you listen to that statement?

SF: Well, at first I just listen.

K: You listen. Do you make an idea of it?

SF: Often, later, yes.

K: No, it's a simultaneous process. You listen and you get an idea of it, and the idea is not the actual observation. That is all I am saying. From the Greeks and the Hindus, our whole structure is based on ideas. And we are saying idea is not actual happening, which is the actual listening.

PM: The idea is just a picture of the actual listening.

K: Yes, which is an evasion, an avoidance of actual observation.

PM: Of the immediate fact.

K: Yes, of looking or listening.

SS: Then there may be something that we are evading constantly.

WR: Yes.

SS: As we've been talking about thought and the various things that it has devised in order to create some kind of freedom or liberation or salvation or redemption, I would like to suggest that there may be some driving factor that is part of thought, or there may be a driving factor that accounts for this, which may be sorrow.

K: Yes, sir, escape from pain through reward.

SS: It seems to apply to all civilizations, both the most sophisticated and the more primitive.

K: Obviously. Because all our thinking is based on these two principles, reward and punishment. Our reward is enlightenment, God, nirvana, or whatever you like to call it, away from anxiety, guilt, all the pain of existence, you know, the misery of it all.

PM: Is it not possible to be free from the idea of reward or punishment?

K: That's what I'm saying. As long as our minds are thinking in terms of reward and punishment, that is time.

PM: How is it that our minds think that way?

K: Because we're educated that way.

PM: Yes, true.

K: We are conditioned from childhood, in the West from the time of the Greeks, because for them measurement was important, otherwise you couldn't have all this technological knowledge.

PM: And would you say that this is due to the fact that we are tied to the idea of a separate "me," a separate "I"? Supposing one sees, hears, touches, and so forth, all in terms of a wholeness, an awareness of wholeness?

K: One can't be aware of the wholeness unless one has understood the movement of thought, because thought is in itself limited.

PM: Thought, yes, of course, which means the intrusion of the self-consciousness as a separate something. Otherwise it won't be there.

K: Sir, how did this self-separative consciousness come into being?

PM: Conditioning in the first instance.

K: It's so obvious.

PM: I, you, me.

K: Of course, measurement.

PM: Measurement, exactly. And analogically that inevitably gets transferred to the realm of the psyche, the realm of the mind.

K: Of course.

PM: Or whatever it is.

K: So we come to this point. You make a statement that man has used psychological time as a means of achieving his reward. It's so obvious. And that reward is away from the pain that he has had. So we are saying that this search for reward, or the achievement of the reward, is a movement of time. And is there such a thing at all? We have invented it, it may be illusion. And from this illusion I can't go to reality—I mean to truth. So the mind must be totally, completely free of this movement of measurement. Is that possible?

PM: As a short answer, I would simply say "Yes."

K: Either you say "Yes" as a logical conclusion, or a speculative assertion, or a desired concept, or it is so.

PM: Yes, an of-courseness is there. If there is a sense of of-courseness, "of course it is so," then there is . . .

K: Then I assume it is so, but I go on for the rest of my life moving in the other direction.

PM: If one really sees . . .

K: Ah, that's what we are saying.

PM: Then one doesn't go in the other direction.

K: So that's what we're saying, do we see it, or is it that we *think* we see it?

PM: Quite.

MZ: Can we go back for a moment? You said you observe, you hear the statement, you observe it. What does the mind actually do in that observation?

K: If I can put it this way—please don't accept what one is saying, but let's find out—observation in the sense of a seeing without naming, without measuring, without a motive, without an end. Obviously that is actually seeing. The very word "idea," from the Greek means "to observe."

MZ: Sir, we would probably all agree with that. But what is acting at that moment? It is a kind of logic, I think, in most people.

K: No.

MZ: What you've said seems very evident.

K: Observation implies silence and not forming any conclusion, just to observe silently, without any psychological or sensory response, except either visual or inward insight, without the responses of memory.

WR: Without any value judgment.

K: Yes.

PM: Would you say, sir, that implies without any reaction from the brain or the senses?

K: Wait, it is a dangerous thing to bring in the brain. Because then we have to go into the whole question of the brain, and I don't want to do that for the moment. It implies that thought is absolutely quiet in observation.

PM: Scientists, for example, who have a really new, remarkable inspiration, or again, great artists when they create wonderful things—this happens when everything is quiet inside, which allows the new to emerge, the truly new, it's a pulse of creation.

K: Yes, sir, but the scientist's insight or perception is partial.

PM: That is to say, the formulation of that insight is partial.

K: Ah, his insight is not only formulation but the very fact of his insight, because insight implies a whole transformation of his daily life; it isn't just "I'm a scientist and I have an insight into mathematics, matter, the atom." Insight implies the way the man lives as a whole.

WR: That is perfectly so.

PM: And any insight is a particular manifestation rooted in the background of the whole.

K: Ah no, we go off into something else there, which is rather confusing. Sir, let us talk a little bit about insight or seeing. Insight implies an observation in which there is no remembrance of things past, therefore the mind is alert, free from all accumulations and so on just to observe. Only then do you have an insight. But that insight we are talking about involves his whole life, not as a scientist, or as an artist. They have partial insight.

WR: That is only a small fragment.

K: A fragment of insight, but that's not what we're talking about.

WR: What we are talking of is the whole of existence.

K: Of course, man's existence.

PM: So in that state of observation that you're talking of, there is no reaction whatsoever.

K: Of course, obviously. It isn't cause-effect reaction.

PM: Quite, it's free of causality.

K: Obviously, otherwise we are back in the old cause being a motive and so on.

WR: And that seeing is beyond time and is not limited or caught in time.

K: That insight is not involved in time.

WR: That's right. And naturally it is neither cause nor effect.

K: Yes, but wait a minute. Have we got this insight into the psychological invention of time by thought as achieving some result? Have you got insight, do you *see* it, or is it just at a verbal, ideological level?

WR: Or whether it is a fact that psychological time is necessary for seeing.

K: No, sir. We went into this question. Man has invented time, psychologically, to achieve a desired end, a purpose, a reward. Does one see this as *an idea*, or is it so? It's so obvious: it is so. Then how is man—this is the point—how is man, a human being, to totally move away from that, totally transform this whole concept of idea, of time? I say it is only possible when you have an insight into this whole thing, which doesn't involve effort, which doesn't involve concentration, all that. This is real meditation.

PM: In fact, it just happens.

K: It is real meditation.

SF: Sir, there is a dilemma that I think many people find themselves in when they listen to that, which is that in order to have this insight . . .

K: Ah, you can't *have* it.

SF: Well, in order for this insight to occur, there must be an insight into thought. And it seems like it's somewhat of a closed circle.

K: No, thought, as we said, is the response of memory, and memory is knowledge, experience, and so thought is moving from the past, always from the past, it is never free from the past.

SF: And we said that there must be a seeing, an observing without . . .

K: Seeing that!

SF: Right. Now we can't see that with thought. We were saying that there must be a seeing, an observing, which is an insight . . .

K: Into thought.

SF: Into thought.

K: Wait, just hold it. Now, thought is the response of memory. Memory, stored in the brain through experience, has become knowledge. So knowledge is always the past, and from that thought arises. This is irrefutable; I mean, this is so. Now is this an idea or an actuality that you yourself have perceived? Do you yourself see that the ascent of man through knowledge is not so? Man can ascend perhaps technologically, but psychologically, if he continues with the accumulation of knowledge, he's caught in the trap. Do you see that? Or do you make it into an idea and say, "What do you mean by it?" and so on.

SF: But, sir, just to see that, I must be free.

K: No, observe, you first listen, without analysis, without inter-pretation, without like or dislike, just listen. And if you so listen, you have absorbed it, absorbed the fact that thought is the re-sponse of memory. Then you can proceed. And can thought then ever free itself from its mother, from its roots, from its source? Obviously not.

SS: But thought can be aware of its own activity.

K: Of course, we went through all that.

MZ: Would you say that if insight comes into being at that moment, then that insight doesn't fall back into the thought mechanism?

K: Oh no, of course not. Say, for instance, you have an insight and you act. Now let's be clear. Insight means instant action, not have an insight and act later. That very insight implies action, and you act. And that action is always right, "right" meaning accurate, precise, without any regret, without any effort, without any reward or punishment: it is so.

SS: But that action is not necessarily doing anything. It may be nonaction in terms of doing things externally.

K: You may have to act both externally and inwardly. If I have an insight into attachment, attachment to ideas, to conclusions, to persons, to my knowledge, to my experience—if I have an insight into that, the whole thing is abandoned.

WR: And may I put it, sir, in another way—I don't know whether you agree—to *see* this illusion.

K: Yes, but one must be sure that it is an illusion.

WR: Whether you call it illusion or whatever name you give it, to see.

K: "What is." That's all.

WR: Yes, see "what is." Don't give it a term.

K: No, to see "what is."

WR: To see "what is" is to see the truth.

K: No, you see, you're bringing in truth—I'm not yet ready for that.

WR: I want to get to it before one o'clock! [*laughter*] I don't want to postpone it, but your main thesis is, don't put in time. To see "what is," as it is, is to see the truth. That's what I would like to put in here, to cut it short. And truth is not somewhere away from . . .

K: Sir, I don't know what it is.

WR: That is what I am saying, to see.

K: I don't know what it means to see. You have told me what it means to see, but I may not see, I may *think* I see.

WR: Yes, then you are not seeing.

K: I must be very clear that I am not *thinking* I'm seeing. Sir, my whole life is that—I *think* I see.

WR: Which is different from seeing.

K: You say so, but ordinary persons say, yes, I see. Which is, I *think* I see what you're saying. But I may not see actually "what is." I *think* I see "what is."

SF: This might be a simple question, but you say that the ordinary person says, "I see what you're saying," but in fact he doesn't. He just sees something mentally or intellectually. Could we say what is going to bring about for the ordinary person this correct seeing, this seeing without thought?

K: I have explained it, sir. First, I must listen. But do we listen, or do we have all kinds of conclusions, our minds so filled with them that they aren't capable of listening? You see me, you say, "He's an Indian, what the heck, get rid of him, he knows nothing." Or you say, "Well, he's considered to be so and so, this or that." So you don't actually listen.

SF: Well, then the question is—I would just change the terminology—what could bring about that correct listening?

K: It has been said, through suffering, which is nonsense. It has been said, make effort, which is nonsense. You listen when somebody says, "I love you," don't you? So can you do the same thing, listen to what you think is unpleasant? [*pause*] So, sir, now come back to this question of truth. Do we have a discussion this afternoon? Can we then pursue truth?

WR: No, I don't want to wait for truth! [*laughter*]

K: You want it all in five minutes, sir?

WR: Not even five minutes.

K: One minute?

WR: One minute. If you can't do it in one minute, you can't do it in five hours.

K: I quite agree. All right, sir, in one second. Truth is not perceivable through time. Truth doesn't exist when the self is there. Truth doesn't come into existence if thought is moving in any direction. Truth is something that cannot be measured. And without love, without compassion, with its own intelligence, truth cannot be.

WR: Yes, now again you have given it in negative terms, in the real tradition of the Buddha.

K: Now you have translated into terms of tradition. Therefore, forgive me for pointing it out, you have moved away from the actual listening to this.

WR: I listened, I listened very well.

K: Then you have captured the perfume of it.

WR: Yes, I have captured the perfume of what you said. And that is why I wanted to have it in one minute.

K: So, sir, what then is the relationship of truth to reality? Be careful. I mean, are these two everlastingly divided?

WR: No.

K: No?

WR: No, I am not hesitating, they are not divided.

K: How do you know?

WR: I know it.

K: "They are not divided." Now, what do you mean by that, sir?

WR: That is what I said, to see.

K: No, just a minute, sir. Truth and reality, you say, are not divided. That means thought and truth are always together. If they are not divided, if something is not divorced, separated, it is together, a unitary movement. Thought . . .

WR: Not thought.

K: Wait, reality, that is why I went into it, sir. Reality is every-thing that thought has put together. We are all agreed that this is so. We may use the terminology, the word "reality," as something else, I don't care, but for the present we are saying, reality is all the things that thought has put together, including illusion. And truth is nothing whatsoever to do with this, it can't be. And there-fore the two cannot be together.

WR: To see that illusion, or whatever it may be, to see "what is," is to see the truth. "What is" is the truth. There is no truth apart from that. "What is" is the truth, what is not is untrue.

K: No, sir, no. We said reality is the movement of thought. Right, sir? And truth is timeless. Truth is timeless, it is not your truth, my truth, his truth—it is something beyond time. Thought is of time, the two cannot run together, that's what I'm saying.

WR: What I said is that there are not two. That is again duality, again you are dividing.

K: No, I'm not. I'm pointing out, sir, I may be mistaken, but I'm just pointing out that thought has created such illusion, and has brought about so much deception, and it may deceive itself by saying, "Yes, I've seen the truth." Therefore I must be very clear, there must be clarity, that there is no deception whatsoever. And I'm saying that deception exists, will inevitably exist, if I don't understand the nature of reality.

WR: I think here we have come to truth.

K: I haven't come to truth, I can't go to truth.

WR: No, you see the truth.

K: I don't see the truth. There's a tremendous difference. I can't go to truth, I can't see truth. Truth can exist only, can be only, or is only, when the self is not.

WR: That is right.

Life after Death

Fifth Conversation with the Buddhist Scholar
Walpola Rahula, and with Phiroz Mehta
and Others

KRISHNAMURTI: Sir, your question was whether there is life after death.

WALPOLA RAHULA: May I say a few words about it? I want to ask you this because, as far as I know, all religions agree in assuming the existence of life after death. Buddhism and Hinduism, of course, assume that there is not just one life, but many lives before and after the present one. That is Hindu and Buddhist teaching. But as far as I know, Christianity considers that there is just one life after death, either in hell or in heaven.

K: Yes, sir, Muslims too.

WR: Muslims too. I don't know very much about the others, but the religions I have mentioned consider that there is life after death. I'm not sure, but I think Zoroastrianism does too. And of course, in all these religions, except Buddhism, there is the soul, self, atman, an unchanging, everlasting, permanent substance in the human being, which transmigrates or is reincarnated. Buddhism does not accept such a self, atman or soul or ego that is eternal, permanent, everlasting, unchanging. Buddhism sees the human being as composed of five psycho-physical aggregates or, to use the Buddhist terms, name and form.

K: Name and form.

WR: Those are terms that you use very often. "Name" means the mental qualities, and "form" is the physical body. But according to Buddhism, these are all energies or forces. And the Buddhist view is that what is called death is the nonfunctioning of the body.

K: Yes.

WR: But that nonfunctioning of the body does not mean the nonfunctioning of all other qualities and energies, like desire, the will to become, to become more and more, and all that. They will continue as long as man is imperfect, so long as he has not seen the truth. Once man sees the truth, he is perfect, and there is no desire for becoming, because there is nothing to become. But while man is imperfect he always has desire and will. And, as you pointed out this morning, he thinks he has time to become more and more perfect and so on.

So for him, because he is not perfect, there is rebirth. But according to Buddhism, whatever continues is not one unchanging substance, but cause and effect, in just the same way, the Buddha says, as we die and are reborn every moment. So in Buddhism it is wrong to say "reincarnation," because there is nothing to incarnate. Neither is "transmigration" a good term. And we often say nowadays "rebirth," which is not quite correct either. The Buddhist term in Pali is *punabhava*, which means re-becoming, the unbroken continuity of becoming. That is the Buddhist view. The question is asked very often, in many Buddhist texts, is it the same person or another person? The traditional and classical Buddhist answer is *Na ca so, na ca anno*—"Neither he nor another." That is the process of continuity, "neither he nor another." A child grows up to be a man of fifty—is he the same person as the child or is he another? He is neither the same person as the child, nor is he another. That is the Buddhist attitude to rebirth.

And now I would like to know, what is your attitude and your interpretation?

K: Sir, could we take a journey together a little bit?

WR: You mean, you would like me to answer, or . . . ?

K: No, journey together, investigating this thing.

WR: Yes.

K: Would you say that all humanity, whether the human being lives in America, Russia, India or Europe, is caught in sorrow, conflict, strife, guilt, a great sense of misery, loneliness, unhappiness, confusion, and that this is the common lot of humanity throughout the world? That is, the consciousness of man—not super-consciousness or some other kind of consciousness, but the content of the ordinary consciousness of man—is all this. Would you agree, sir?

WR: Yes.

K: Human beings—I won't say "man," because there are a lot of girls here too—human beings, throughout the world, share the same psychological phenomena. Outwardly they may differ, being tall, short, dark, and so on, but psychologically they are greatly similar. So one can say, you are the world. Would you?

PHIROZ MEHTA: Entirely.

K: Would you agree to that, sir? You are the world, and the world is you. Right, sir? Let's talk about it.

WR: Yes, in a sense.

K: No, not in a sense, not partially, it is so. You are born in

Ceylon, he was born in India, another is born in America or in Europe, or on this island, England. Outwardly, one's culture, tradition, climate, food, all that may vary. But inwardly we have the same sense of guilt, not about something, but the feeling of guilt, the feeling of anxiety. Right?

WR: Yes, I would say anxiety rather than guilt, the feeling of guilt arises in a certain kind of society.

K: I mean it's guilt: unless you are insensitive, brutal, one feels guilty. But that's a minor point.

STEPHEN SMITH: Perhaps guilt is more prevalent in the Western tradition, and something more like shame in the East.

K: In the East they translate it differently.

SS: But the feeling is the same.

K: It is karma, or their lot, and so on. All right, I won't use "guilt." Let us say "anxiety."

WR: Yes, anxiety.

K: Loneliness, despair, various forms of depression, sorrow, and fear, these are the common lot of man. That's obvious. The consciousness of human beings is made up of its content, and the content is all this, and human beings throughout the world are more or less similar, apart from their physical name and form. Would you agree?

WR: Yes.

K: So one can say, not as a verbal statement but as a fact, that we human beings are alike. And so, deeply, you are me.

WR: There is similarity.

K: That's what I'm saying. And I am you.

WR: Yes, we are similar.

K: Because everyone goes through various forms of hell, tragedy, misfortune. And so the world, humanity, is one. Would you agree?

PM: Humanity is one.

K: If you see that, accept it, then what is death? Who is it that dies? The name, the form, and also the anxiety, the pain, the sorrow, the misery—does that also die? You're following my point, sir? Can we discuss this a little? That is, to me the world is actually the "me," it is not just words. I am the world. I may have different physical contours, physical facial differences, height and color and so on, but we are not considering that. Psychologically we go through extraordinary misery, tragedy and ugliness, hurt. So that is the common consciousness of man. That is the stream— psychologically—in which man lives. Right?

If you really accept that, or see it as being real, not imagined or idealistic, but as a fact, then what is it to die? If you accept that fact, then what is death, what is it that dies? The body, the form, the name? The form and the name may be different from you, you are a man, she is a woman, and all the rest of it. But that is the common stream in which humanity lives, with occasional spurts of happiness, rare moments of great joy, rare moments of a sense of great beauty. That is our common life, this vast stream is going on all the time. It's a great river. Let's discuss this, you may disagree completely.

MARY ZIMBALIST: Sir, are you saying that in that stream the whole notion of some individual consciousness, which most people share, is a complete illusion?

K: I think so.

MZ: Why does mankind invariably have that illusion?

K: Because it's part of our education, part of our culture, both religious and worldly, that you are an individual, you know, the whole idea of it. Although the word "individual" is really misapplied, because "individual" means one who is indivisible. But we are all broken up. So we can hardly call ourselves individuals.

PM: We are fragmented.

K: We are fragmented, broken up. So if we see that man's consciousness is the consciousness of the world, of . . .

PM: All humanity.

K: Of all humanity, in that vast river which has no beginning, which is still going on. And I and another are part of that stream. I and another die. What happens to all my desires, to all my anxieties, fears, longings, aspirations, the enormous burden of sorrow which I have carried for years—what happens to all that, when the body dies?

PM: It commingles with the world stream.

K: It is part of that stream.

PM: Exactly.

MZ: It was never yours at all.

K: It's not mine, it's part of that stream, which has manifested itself as K, with his form. Sir, what I'm saying is very drastic compared to what all the religions say.

WR: Now I would raise a question. In that stream there is K . . .

K: Wait! There is no K. That is the whole point. There is only that stream, which is made up of desire, anxiety, despair, loneliness, all the travail of mankind. That is the river.

PM: As well as their opposites, the opposites of pain and so on.

K: My pleasure, which lasts for a few days, and which I then pursue, and cry if I can't get again. And feeling flattered if I'm rewarded. That is also part of that vast river.

PM: Would you say, sir, that because of our ignorance, that which we call the individual is a misnomer?

K: It is not only a misnomer, I don't think it exists. You have a separate name and a bank account, but your consciousness is like that of everyone else.

PM: But if we say that it doesn't exist at all, then we would have to say that humanity also doesn't exist.

K: No, I'm going to go into it. So if we see that, if we see it not only logically, reasonably, but factually, that it is so—that you were born in India and I was born in Europe, or in America, but we go through the same hell, through the same rat race.

MZ: So, may one—just to be sure so far, so that it's clear—say there is nothing apart from that in the human . . . ?

K: Wait, I'm coming to that. In that stream, human beings have invented gods, rituals, the saviors, the Virgin Mary, Krishnas, all of whom are part of that stream. They've invented these.

MZ: But apart from the inventions, the illusions, is there any other something?

K: Yes, is there anything spiritual? I understand. Is there anything that is not of time?

MZ: That is not of the stream.

K: Is there in the stream anything which is not man-made? Let's call it that for the moment. Is that what you're asking?

MZ: I'm not sure. Is there something that is not of the stream in the human mind, human consciousness, whatever you want to call it?

K: Man has invented something.

MZ: No, not an invention, something real.

K: Not in that stream, not in that river.

MZ: I'm not asking if there's something else in the river, I'm asking if there's something else in man except the river.

K: Nothing. No atman, no soul, no God, nothing. Don't accept it, please.

MZ: There is an enormous implication in that.

K: There is a tremendous implication.

MZ: Because if that were so there would be no end to the stream.

K: No, the man who steps out—but I don't want to go further at this stage, I want to go slowly, step by step. Is that so, that for all human beings, their common consciousness is made up of this vast river? Right, sir? You may not accept this.

WR: I'm not accepting or rejecting, I am thinking about it, meditating. What Mary said was a very important point.

K: Yes, we'll answer that presently.

WR: Is there no escape from the stream?

K: I'm going to answer it presently—it is not escape.

WR: Or whatever it may be.

K: But we are considering death. So that stream is common to all of us, our consciousness is of that stream.

SHAKUNTALA NARAYAN: Are you saying, sir, that thought is common to all of us, because all this is a creation and manifestation of thought?

K: Yes, thought, not only the creation of thought, but the creation of illusions by thought.

SN: And the operation of those illusions.

K: And the operation of those illusions—Christian, Buddhist, Muslim, Hindu; British, French, Russian, various ideologies—all that is part of this stream.

PM: May I ask, sir, is it a case of thought as it is functioning here with us now, which has created these illusions, or is it that mind as a universal constituent, as a universal factor in the process of thinking through what we commonly call the particular person, releases these ideas?

K: Let's go a little bit slowly. I want this to be clear, that we are part of that stream.

PM: Yes, that is so.

K: And when the body dies, the desires, the anxieties, the trage-dies, and the misery go on. I die, and that stream, that river goes on. Right, sir, or do you reject this? I don't see how you can re-ject it.

WR: No rejection, no acceptance.

K: No, just wait—right?

WR: Only waiting for the conclusion.

K: Quite right. So that river manifests itself as K.

WR: Not the whole river.

K: The river, which is desire, the river is that.

PM: One of its manifestations is K.

K: The river manifests, not one of the manifestations.

PM: Well then, how does . . .

K: No, sorry. I'll make it a bit clear. The river manifests itself as K. That's agreed.

WR: Then the river also manifests as R.

K: No, wait. The river manifests itself as K. And K has certain capacities by tradition, by education and so on, to paint, to build a marvelous cathedral. But we're talking psychologically. Look, sir, let's go back to it. We agree that the river is that.

WR: I don't know.

K: What do you mean, sir, you don't know?

WR: I fully agree that the whole of humanity without excep-tion . . .

K: Is one.

WR: Everything that you have described as suffering, all of that is common to all humanity. In that sense, we are all equal, but not all one.

K: No equality or anything. We are of that stream.

WR: Yes, that's right.

K: I am the representative of all mankind. Me, because I am of that stream.

WR: Well, that I don't know.

GIDDU NARAYAN: It's a qualitative thing.

K: What do you mean by qualitative?

GN: When you say, "I am of that stream," all the qualities of the stream are in me.

K: Yes, that's right.

GN: Not that I'm the whole river, but the drop contains all the qualities of the river.

WR: Yes.

K: But the river is that.

MZ: Would it be helpful to use the example of a wave, which is no different from the rest of the ocean?

K: Yes.

MZ: But it manifests as a wave that disappears.

K: If you like to put it that way. But this must be clear. Each one of us is the representative of all mankind, because one is the representative of that stream, and mankind is of that stream, therefore each one of us is the representative of the whole of that stream.

WR: That is better.

K: You allow that. So, let's go. And that stream manifests itself as K, or as X, forget K. It manifests itself as X with a form and name, but that stream also has the quality of containing within it art, there is everything in there.

WR: Not only X, there is Y.

K: Dozens, X, Y, Z.

WR: Yes, that's what I want to make clear.

K: As long as mankind is in that stream, and one manifestation of that stream leaves the stream, in his case he is completely free of that stream.

WR: So you are not the whole of humanity, because if you leave the river, then the whole of humanity leaves it.

K: Just a minute, sir, just a minute. That stream has manifested in X, and if X in that manifestation doesn't free himself completely from the stream, he is back in it.

MZ: But, sir, this is the moment that the earlier question referred to.

K: I'm coming to that.

MZ: What is there? You said there was nothing separate from the stream.

K: Wait, I haven't explained it yet. There is nothing, there is that stream, right? It manifests itself as A. In that manifestation, with all the educational and environmental influences and so on, if that A doesn't step out of that stream, there is no salvation for mankind.

MZ: Sir, what is there to step out?

K: Leave, finish with your anxieties, sorrow, all the rest of it.

MZ: But you said there was nothing except the content of the stream.

K: As long as I remain in the stream.

MZ: What is the "I"?

K: "I" is the thing that has manifested itself as A, and A now calls himself individual, which is not factual, which is illusory. But when A dies, he is part of that stream. That's clear.

MZ: Yes, but if A is composed of the water of the stream . . .

K: Yes.

MZ: How can the water of the stream step out of the stream?

K: Oh yes.

PARCHURE: So there is some logical error in our . . .

K: In my explanation.

P: Yes. Once you say that you are the representative of mankind, humanity, which is the . . .

K: Is that so or not?

P: Yes.

K: Don't say "Yes," sir. Aren't you the representative of the whole of mankind, psychologically?

WR: I think that is too general and too vague a statement.

K: No, it's not vague. I have made it very clear. That stream is this content of our consciousness, which is agony, pain, desire, strife, all that.

WR: That is common to all of us. In that sense, all humanity is equal or one. But I can't accept your attitude, your position, that I am humanity.

K: Of course, if I accept that stream, I'm part of that stream, therefore I am like the rest of humanity.

WR: *Like* the rest.

K: I said that, therefore a representative of all of that stream.

WR: That also I accept.

K: That's all I'm saying.

WR: But you can't say, "I am that stream, the whole stream."

K: No, I am that stream.

MZ: But, sir, maybe we're being literal, but there's a concept in this somewhere of a sort of container which contains the stream.

K: No, not ships that carry containers and all that. Don't bring in containers!

MZ: But what is it that can separate itself from the stream if it is only made up of the water of the stream?

K: Part of that stream is this egotistic concept. That's all.

MZ: No, but what can separate? How can water divide itself from the ocean?

K: You're missing my whole point.

WR: Her point is this: What is it that steps out of the river? That is the question.

K: Wait. If *that* is the question, I'll answer it presently, I'll answer it. I'm pretty good at this!—I'm only joking, this is much too serious. You see, when you ask that question, "What is it that steps out?" you are implying, positing an otherness, something that is not of the stream. Right?

WR: Or rather, *you* are positing this.

K: I'm not. I haven't posited anything at all, I've only stated what is actually happening. I won't posit anything. I've said, as long as man does not step out of that stream, there is no salvation for mankind. That's all.

PM: Sir, may I add a word here. I think the question that the lady asked implies an identifiable permanent entity.

K: There is no permanent entity.

PM: No, what I'm suggesting is . . .

MZ: A something, I'm not making it more definite than that.

K: I know what you're trying to say.

MZ: There has to be X or—I don't know what to call it.

GN: Some aspect of intelligence.

K: That's what he's saying.

MZ: Something that can step out of the stream.

K: Yes, is there some aspect of intelligence in the stream?

GN: Yes, which sees the futility of the stream.

K: Which sees the . . . yes, and therefore steps out.

MZ: Then you're saying that quality is part of the stream, it's in with all the other human things, something is able . . .

K: Just a minute.

MZ: To separate itself from all the rest of the stream.

K: A is part of that stream. Let's go step by step, if you don't mind, then we won't mislead each other. A is part of that stream. That stream has manifested itself as A. So A perceives he's suffering. Obviously. Right?

GN: Yes.

K: He is living, he feels anxiety, and he says, "Why am I suffering? What is this?" And so he begins to reason, he begins to see. Why do you introduce some other factor?

MZ: Can you then say that it is some perception that is still part of the stream?

K: No.

MZ: Or some molecule, or something.

K: No, you are not listening, if you don't mind my pointing out.

WR: May I add a word, sir?

K: Yes, sir.

WR: According to the Buddha's teaching, there is also, in that stream, wisdom which sees the whole thing. Buddhist philosophy explains this very clearly. It is the answer to Mary's question.

GN: Which sees what?

WR: The whole thing, which sees reality, which sees it as it is, as we discussed this morning. And then that seeing is the stepping out.

MZ: Are you saying that there is an action of stepping out without an actor?

K: Yes, go with me, I'll explain it. I'll explain it, but you don't have to accept it. I think it'll be logical, reasonable, and fairly sane, and unless one is completely besotted, it can be examined. A is of that stream, with a name and a form, and as he lives, he realizes what he is going through. In that realization he says, "I'm suffering." Then he begins to inquire into the whole nature of suffering, and ends that suffering. I'm taking one aspect of this stream. He ends that suffering. And he is out of that stream. That entity who is out of that stream is really unique.

SCOTT FORBES: So it's something there that wasn't there before?

K: The moment A realizes that he's suffering, and doesn't escape from that suffering, but inquires into and explores without any motive and so on the nature of suffering, and has an insight into the whole structure of suffering, that very insight ends that suffering.

WR: That insight is also in the stream.

K: You see, just a moment—you're positing something that I am not.

WR: Where are you bringing insight from?

K: I brought in insight very carefully. A realizes he's suffering. Suffering is part of that stream.

WR: A is also part of the stream.

K: Yes, that stream has manifested itself in A. A, living, realizes he is suffering, he doesn't escape from it, because he wants to know the whole nature and structure of, and what is behind, suffering. So he examines it both logically, sanely, and also nonverbally. He looks into it, and the very looking into it is the insight. The looking into the suffering is not of the stream.

WR: Where does that "looking into" come from?

K: As I have said, he is concerned, he is studying, exploring, questioning the whole beastly thing—he wants to know.

WR: That means it is not a part of the river.

K: No.

SF: But, Krishnaji, we've been saying that something steps out of the river . . .

K: Wait, I won't use that expression "stepping out."

SF: And it seems now that what we're saying is that something comes into being which was never part of that river.

K: Just follow me, and see if I'm wrong, then correct me. A is of that stream, A is suffering, A says, "Why?" He's not concerned with what the teacher has said; he says, "I know all that," he pushes all that aside. Why is there suffering? In the very inquiry into it—the inquiry depends on your capacity to put aside interpretation, to not escape, and all the rest of it—in the very inquiry into the nature of suffering, and the cause and effect of it, and so on, in that very inquiry comes insight. Insight isn't in the stream.

SF: Right.

WR: I say it is in the stream.

K: Why, sir?

WR: You see, it has in itself the capacity of producing and ceasing.

K: The stream itself has the capacity?

WR: Of continuing and producing and stopping it. That insight is also part of that stream, just as all the misery is.

K: No, sir, I wouldn't . . .

WR: Then where does that insight come from?

K: I'm telling you, sir.

WR: You say A is part of the river?

K: Yes, A is suffering. A begins to inquire, A begins to—wait—in his inquiry he realizes inquiry can only exist when there's complete freedom from all escapes, suppression and all the rest of it. So in that moment of inquiry there is insight. When he doesn't escape, when he doesn't suppress, when he doesn't rationalize or seek the cause of suffering, in that very moment of examining is insight.

GN: You're implying insight is born, and it is not of the stream.

K: Don't introduce born, not of the stream. You see, you are misleading, you want it to be part of that stream.

GN: Where does insight come from, then?

K: I'm telling you.

GN: From inquiry.

K: From the freedom to inquire.

GN: Where does that freedom to inquire come from?

K: From his own examination.

WR: But he is part of the river.

K: No, you're missing the point.

SF: Krishnaji, are we saying this, that A normally is nothing more than a name and a form, plus all that there is in the river? And with free inquiry . . .

K: A begins to inquire.

SF: Right, A begins to inquire and then A, if he has this insight . . .

K: No, "he" does not have the insight.

SF: He is no longer just a part of that river.

K: Would you just follow, step by step? A is part of that stream, A is the manifestation of that stream, a wave of that stream, or whatever you like to call it. Now A is going through agony. A examines it. And the examination is very important, because if he escapes, it is not examination, not exploration. If he suppresses, it is not. So he realizes—please follow this step by step—that as long as he's not free from the blockages, this prevents exploration, and therefore he puts them aside, he's free to inquire. And in that freedom is insight.

P: There is a missing link here.

K: There may be ten, sir.

P: It appears from what G. Narayan was saying that if the person is part of the stream, a representative of the stream, then when inquiry begins, examination starts, freedom comes . . .

K: Be careful, sir. No, you see, you are assuming so much.

P: No, but I'm repeating what you're saying.

K: Yes, all right, you're repeating what I said.

P: And the beginning of this, the beginning of inquiry, the beginning of the capacity to explore without any of the things of the stream, are they also in the stream?

K: No.

P: Where do they come from?

K: That's very simple. What are you all making a fuss about?

P: This beginning of the inquiry is . . .

K: No, forgive me, Doctor, you're not listening. I said that A is the manifestation of that stream. Let's follow it step by step. Part of that stream is suffering. A is suffering, so A says, "Why should I suffer?"

P: At this point I will interrupt you.

K: At any point.

P: So whatever the number of human beings in the stream, the question "Why should I suffer?" is the beginning of the whole thing.

K: No, the human being has asked, "Why should I suffer?" and there are a dozen explanations—the Buddhist, the Hindu, the Christian and so on. The person who is suffering says, "I see all this, the Buddhist, the Hindu, the Christian, the Muslim explanations, I reject all that, because that doesn't leave me the freedom to inquire. I won't accept tradition and authority."

PM: Sir, perhaps we could put it this way. That the conditioned inquiry . . .

K: Is part of the stream.

PM: Is part of the stream.

K: That's the whole point.

PM: But the free inquiry . . .

K: Is the beginning of . . .

GN: Getting away from the stream.

K: No, leave the stream alone now! A is the manifestation of that stream, A is suffering, A says, "Why am I suffering?" He studies Buddhism, studies Hinduism, studies Christianity, and says, "For God's sake, that world is out. I'm going to find out for myself." And he begins to inquire. And he realizes he can only explore if he is free to look. Right? Free from fear, free from reward and punishment, free from any kind of motive, otherwise he can't inquire. The moment he is in that state of examination, there is insight. This is very clear.

PM: And of course very difficult to do.

K: No, I won't even accept the word "difficult."

PM: At first, because otherwise we wouldn't be inquiring.

K: No, because we have not given our energy to this. We don't care, we have put up with so many things. Now put A aside. B is part of that stream, and he suffers, he says, "Yes, that's my nature, that's human nature, there is no way out, no Jesus, nobody is going to save me, I'll put up with it." So he is contributing to the stream.

SS: So the stream becomes more intense.

K: Yes, it has more volume.

PM: More drive also.

K: Of course, more volume, the pressure of tremendous water. So we come to the point: What is death?

WR: I want to put another question. Now A is out of the river.

K: No, sir, A is not out of the river.

WR: But he has seen, had insight.

K: He has insight.

WR: Insight. So if A is the whole of humanity, then humanity has seen it.

K: No, sir.

MZ: So he has left humanity.

PM: You are looking at it, perhaps, purely logically.

K: No, not even logically.

PM: What I mean is, logically but accepting the conditioned states.

K: The moment A is aware of his conditioned state and begins to inquire into it, he has got the energy to put it aside.

PM: Now the Buddha himself said, "Put aside with right wisdom"—do you remember that phrase of the Buddha? "Put aside all shape and form, all sensation, all perceptions, all discriminative consciousness itself."

WR: That's what I say.

PM: Put it aside with right wisdom.

WR: That is what I tell you. That is what I said, that he is making this so complicated.

PM: No.

K: We're all making it complicated. It is very simple.

WR: That is what I tell you, that is the statement, that is the idea, but I also . . .

K: May I interrupt here? Say one doesn't belong to any religion. One doesn't accept any authority. That is to inquire. If I have accepted what Christ or X Y Z said, it's no inquiry. So in his inquiry into sorrow A rejects everything that anybody had said. Will you do that? Because otherwise he's a secondhand human being, examining through secondhand eyeglasses.

WR: Or you can hear somebody who has seen it and . . .

K: I hear what the Buddha has said. What anybody has said.

WR: Yes, you can hear it. What the Buddha has said, and you can also see independently as he has seen.

K: Yes, Buddha said that sorrow is the beginning of . . . whatever it was he said.

WR: Yes.

K: All right, but "what he said" is not by me.

WR: Absolutely, that is so. That is what I am saying, but you also can see the same thing as he has seen.

K: Yes.

WR: And still you know what he has also said.

K: Sir, to a hungry man the printed word or hearsay has no meaning.

WR: That is so.

K: Reading the menu doesn't feed me.

WR: That is what I'm saying too, it is not the menu but the food.

K: But the food is not cooked by anybody else, I have to cook it, eat it.

WR: That is not usually so.

K: Wait, I said the man who is examining the whole structure of sorrow.

WR: I would put it the other way round, that you have to eat to get rid of hunger. Just because *you* have eaten, *my* hunger will not disappear. You have prepared the food, you have eaten, and there is food. I too can eat it, and it is my food. Do you deny that?

K: No, of course not, sir. This afternoon, you've eaten lunch, somebody cooked it, and we ate it. But we're not talking about food. We are saying that, as long as I accept any authority, it doesn't matter who it is, there is no insight.

WR: No, it does not happen by accepting authority.

K: Accepting descriptions, accepting conclusions, what Buddha said, what Krishna said, or what A said. To me freedom is from the known. Otherwise I shall be everlastingly living in the stream. You see, that is why, sir, either we discuss this factually, and say, "Look, I will drop every authority I have," which means knowledge and tradition, or we do not. Can you do that? Because that is inquiry, whereas if I am tethered to a tradition, I can't: I'll go round in circles. So I must be free of the post and the rope that ties me to the post. [*pause*] But B accepts suffering. Right, sir? B accepts what he is; conditioned, miserable, and unhappy. You know what the human being is. So he is all the time contributing to the stream. So there is no soul, no atman, no ego, no permanent me that evolves. Then what would the inquiry be, what is the state of the mind of the man, of the human who has had an insight into the whole nature of suffering and therefore the whole stream? What is the nature of that mind? What is the quality? Would that be speculative? It would.

SS: Sir, what is the position of the person who has some insight or a partial insight? He's still in there, isn't he?

K: Like the scientist, who has a partial insight. You know, he may be excellent at science, but confused, miserable, unhappy, ambitious.

PM: Don't you think that the very term "partial insight" means a conditioned insight?

K: Of course.

PM: And therefore it is part of that stream and it's true to type generally.

K: I wonder if we see this, sir, or if what we are seeing is an image? Because now we have created the image of the river.

PM: Yes, that's the unfortunate thing.

MZ: Sir, is there a difference between insight and intelligence?

K: Now wait a minute, let us go into that. The stream manifesting itself as B, and in his activities B becomes very cunning and clever. Now, is intelligence wholly unrelated to cunning, cleverness, chicanery, all that, but essentially part of love and compassion? What do you say, sir? The love in the stream is not love. You know, we are saying things that nobody will accept. If B is in the stream, and tells his wife or girlfriend, or she tells her husband or boyfriend, "I love you," is that love?

WR: As long as there is "me," there is no love.

K: No, don't reduce it to the "me." B is of that stream and says to his girlfriend or boyfriend, "I love you"—now, is that love?

WR: In what sense? Love has hundreds of meanings.

K: So that is what I'm inquiring into. The love of a book, the love of your particular soup, the love of poetry, the love of a beautiful thing, the love of an ideal, the love of your country, jealous love, in which is included hate, envy, hurt. Is all that—I'm questioning, exploring this—is all that love? And B is a man who says, "Yes, that is love. At least it's part of love." Or he says, "Without jealousy there is no love." I've heard these statements a dozen times.

WR: Not only that, people have asked me how there can be love without the idea of self.

K: Yes, you see, sir, are we discussing all this verbally? Or realizing, seeing the stream is you, and saying, "Look, examine, end it." And so not being able to end it, we invent time—one day I will step out of that stream. So thought invents psychological evolution.

PM: Could we also say that thought invents psychological development through time?

K: Yes, sir, that is what I mean.

PM: Instead of what really belongs to the psychological sphere, namely immediacy.

K: That's right. The immediacy only takes place when there is insight. In that there is no regret, no saying, "I wish I hadn't done it." But our action is always at the level of time. [*pause*] Sir, what is immortality? What is eternity? What is the immeasurable? All religions touch on this more or less, even the metaphysicians and the logicians and the monks have gone into this. What is immortality? That is, an author writes a good book, and it and his name become immortal. Or a politician's does—unfortunately politicians last, endure. We have related immortality as something beyond death—the mortal and the beyond mortality, beyond death. No?

PM: That's the usual conception.

K: Of course. Well, sir, what do you say to all this?

WR: What happened to our question?

K: About death, rebirth?

WR: Yes, what happened there?

K: I've told you. Rebirth is this constant stream, manifesting itself into A, B, C, down the alphabet. I know this is most disappointing, depressing, and I say, "My God, this is too horrible, I won't listen to it."

SS: Are you also suggesting therefore that death is part of that stream?

K: Yes, the body dies. By usage and a wrong way of living, it inevitably dies.

SS: But I meant something more.

K: You see, sir, to find out what death is, one has to be *with* death. That means *end*. End one's attachments and beliefs, end *everything* that one has collected. Nobody wants to do that.

MZ: But that definition, that action of death would not be in or part of the stream.

K: No, you see, in the man who has gone, who has understood this, he doesn't even think in terms of streams, it is something entirely different. It is not a reward for the man in the stream.

MZ: No, it's the action of the insight, is it not?

K: Yes, the action of insight, and you cannot have insight if there is no love, compassion, intelligence, that's a part of all that. And it is only then there is a relationship to truth.

SS: You seem to be suggesting in some way that death is a key.

K: Yes, sir. Free investigation, not scientific investigation, the think tank, but investigation into this whole myself, the "me," that stream, myself is that stream. Inquire into that, so that there isn't a shadow of the stream left. We don't do this because we are too learned, we have no time, we are too occupied with our own pleasures, our own worries. So we say, "Please, leave that to the priests; it's not for me."

So have we answered the question? Is there reincarnation, a continuation, of the "me" in different forms? I say, no!

WR: Of course not, of course not. Like you, I also say there is not. First of all, there is no "me" to be reborn.

K: No, sir, the stream manifests and B says, "I am I," therefore I'm frightened to die.

WR: Yes.

K: And therefore he invents various comforting theories, he prays, Please save me and all the rest of it. But as long as B lives in that stream, his consciousness is part of that stream, he is only contributing more and more to the volume of the water. Obviously, sir, if you see that. So there is no "me" to continue. Sir, nobody will accept this, but it's the truth.

PM: You would agree, then, that what is necessary is to see in this profound way.

K: Yes, seeing is that.

PM: Truly see, and that truly seeing is real action, creative action.

K: It is action. The moment I see, I drop anxiety, the moment I see I am petty-minded, it is finished.

PM: It is a complete transformation of the ordinary psychical process.

K: Yes.

MZ: Isn't really the crux in all this, and the place where people go wrong, so to speak, that they do not see in the sense that you are talking about; they see verbally, intellectually, on various levels, but they don't really see.

K: No, I think that mostly they don't mind being sorrowful, they say, "Well, why not?" They don't see, one doesn't see, one's own petty reactions. They say, "Yes, why not?"

MZ: Or they don't see that they don't see, to put it perhaps childishly. They don't realize that what they think is understanding is not.

K: No, Maria, I mean—not you personally, has one dropped any opinion that one holds? One's prejudice *completely*? Or one's experience? Never. They say, "Please"—they won't even listen to you. Do you mean to say a politician will listen to you? Or a priest, or anybody who is absolutely caught in his own conclusion? Because there he is completely safe, completely secure. And if you come and disturb him, either he worships you or kills you, which is the same thing.

MZ: Or he sees that such security is a complete fabrication.

K: Then he drops these prejudices, his conclusions, even his knowledge.

SF: Sir, for the man who has stepped out of the stream and is no longer a manifestation of the stream, there is something else that is operating. Could we say something about the nature of that?

K: Which is intelligence. Intelligence is love, intelligence is compassion.

SF: And from many things that you have said in the past that seems to have an independent existence.

K: Obviously.

SF: Without it manifesting in him.

K: Sir, if A frees himself—not himself—if A's consciousness is no longer of the stream, his consciousness is entirely different, of a different dimension altogether.

SF: And that consciousness existed before he stepped out of the stream, so to speak?

K: Now you are speculating.

SF: Yes, I am.

K: I won't play with you. [*laughter*]

SS: Perhaps another way to say it would be, is there intelligence without the intelligent person?

K: I know what you are saying. That means— let us put it round the other way—wars have created a great deal of misery. Right? And that misery must remain in the air. Goodness has been also part of man—trying to be good. So there is an enormous reservoir of both. No?

SS: Yes.

K: So, what? One doesn't contribute to that goodness, but one is always contributing to the other.

MZ: Are you saying the other exists only in the human psyche, but goodness exists apart from humanity?

K: Let's put it round this way: there is not only the suffering of A, there is the suffering of the whole of mankind.

MZ: Or more than mankind, there is suffering.

K: There is suffering, of course.

SS: Suffering is a universal phenomenon.

K: [*turning to Walpola Rahula*] Sir, would you kindly explain what Buddhist meditation is?

WR: Buddhist meditation has taken on many forms, there are many varieties, but the purest form of Buddhist meditation is insight into "what is."

K: You are using my words.

WR: No, these are not your words. *You* are using those words! Long before you, two thousand five hundred years ago, these words were used. And I am using them now.

K: All right, then we are both two thousand years old!

WR: *Vipassana* is insightful vision, to see into the nature of things, that is the real vision.

K: Have they a system?

WR: A system has of course developed.

K: That's what I want to get at.

WR: Yes, but when you take the original teaching of the Buddha . . .

K: . . . there is no system.

WR: The best discourse by the Buddha on this insight meditation is called *Satipatthana*. There is no system.

K: I am listening, sir.

WR: And the key point in that is awareness, *sati* in Pali, *smriti* in Sanskrit. And to be mindful, aware, of all that happens, you are not expected to run away from life and live in a cave or in a forest, sitting like a statue, all that. It is not that. And *satipatthana* is sometimes translated as the establishment of mindfulness, but the precise meaning of the word is the presence of awareness, aware-ness of every movement, every action, everything.

K: Is this awareness to be cultivated?

WR: There is no question of cultivating it.

K: That is what I am trying to get at. Because the modern gurus, with the modern systems of meditation, modern Zen, you know all the rest of it, are trying to cultivate it.

WR: Yes, I have written an essay, to be published in Belgium in honor of Monseigneur Etienne Lamotte, on Buddhist meditation. And there I have said that this teaching of the Buddha has for many centuries been misunderstood and wrongly applied as a tech-nique. And it has been developed into such a technique that in-stead of liberating the mind it can imprison it.

K: Of course, all meditation . . .

WR: If it is made into a system. .

K: Please, sir, is awareness something to be cultivated in the sense of manipulated, watched over, worked at?

WR: No, not at all.

K: So how does it come into being?

WR: There is no coming into being, you do it.

K: Wait, sir, just listen. I want to find out, I am not being criti-cal, I just want to find out what Buddhist meditation is. Because nowadays there are various types of Buddhist meditation, various types of Tibetan meditation, Hindu meditation, Sufi meditation—for God's sake, you follow, they are like mushrooms all over the place. I am just asking if awareness is something that takes place through concentration?

WR: No, not in that sense. For anything we do in this world a certain amount of concentration is necessary. That is understood, but don't let us mix up awareness with *dhyana* and *samadhi*.

K: Personally I don't like any of those words.

WR: They are based essentially on concentration.

K: I know. Most of the meditations that have been propagated all over the world involve concentration.

WR: Concentration is central in Zen and various other practices, in Buddhist or Hindu *samadhis* and *dhyanas*.

K: That is nonsense, I don't accept concentration.

WR: But in the Buddha's pure teaching, meditation is not that concentration.

K: It is not concentration, let us put it that way. Then what is this awareness, how does it come into being?

WR: You are aware, aware of what happens. One great thing in the *Satipatthana* is that you live in the action in the present moment.

K: Wait, sir, you say the present moment, but you don't live in the present moment.

WR: That is what it says, that you don't live in the present moment. And *satipatthana* is to live in the present moment.

K: How is one to live in the present? What is the mind that lives in the present?

WR: The mind that lives in the present is the mind that is free . . .

K: Yes, sir, go on sir, I am waiting, I want to find out.

WR: From the idea of self. When you have the idea of self, either you live in the past or in the future.

K: The now is generally, as far as I—one sees, not "I"—the past modifying itself in the present and going on.

WR: That is the usual situation.

K: Wait, that is the present.

WR: No.

K: Then what is the present? Free of the past?

WR: Yes.

K: That's it. Free of the past, which means free of time. So that is the only state of mind which is now. Now I am just asking, sir, what is awareness? How does it flower, how does it happen? You follow?

WR: There is no technique for it.

K: I understand.

WR: You were asking how it happens, then you are asking for a method.

K: Quite right. I used "how" just to ask a question, not for a method. I'll put it round the other way. In what manner does this awareness come into being? Suppose I am not aware, I am just enclosed in my own petty little worries and anxieties, problems, I love you and you don't love me, and all that is going on in my mind. I live in that. And you come along and tell me, "Be aware of all that." And I say, "What do you mean by being aware?"

WR: When you ask me that, be aware of that pettiness.

K: Yes. So that means be aware . . .

WR: Of the pettiness.

K: Yes, be aware of all your pettiness. What do you mean by that?

WR: Be aware of that.

K: Yes, sir, I don't know how to be, I don't know what it means.

WR: It is not necessary to know what it means.

K: What do you mean, it is not necessary?

WR: Be aware of it.

K: You tell me, be aware of it. But I am blind, I think that is an elephant, how am I to—you follow? I am blind, and I want to see light. And you say, "Be aware of that blindness." I say, "Yes, but what does it mean?" It is not concentration. So I say, Look, awareness is something in which choice doesn't exist. Wait, sir. Awareness means to be aware of this hall, the curtains, the lights, the people sitting here, the shape of the walls, the windows, to be aware of it. Just a minute. Either I am aware of one part, part by part, or as I enter the room I am aware of the whole thing: the roof, the lamps, the curtains, the shape of the windows, the floor, the mottled roof, everything. Is that what you mean, sir?

WR: That too is a kind of awareness.

K: That is awareness. Now what is the difference—I am not categorizing, please I am not being impudent, or inquisitive, or insulting—what is the difference between that sense of awareness and attention?

WR: It is wrong to say "sense of awareness." There is just awareness.

K: All right, that awareness and attention. You see we have abolished concentration, except when I have to drill a hole in the wall, then I hope I am drilling it straight, I concentrate.

WR: We have not excluded it. There is concentration, but that is not the main thing.

K: No, that is not awareness.

WR: But concentration may be useful or helpful.

K: To drill a straight hole.

WR: Yes, in awareness also it may be helpful, but concentration is not the central point.

K: There must be a certain sense of concentration if I have to learn mathematics.

WR: For anything, sir.

K: Therefore I am just putting that aside for the moment. What is attention? To attend.

WR: How do you explain and discriminate between, for instance, awareness, mindfulness, and attention?

K: I would say in awareness there is no choice, just to be aware. The moment when choice enters into awareness, there is no awareness. And choice is measurement, division, and so on. So awareness is without choice, just to be aware. Saying I don't like or I like this room, all that has ended. In attention, to attend, in that attention there is no division.

WR: That also means no choice.

K: Let us leave that for the moment. Attention implies no division, no "me" attending. And so it has no division, therefore no measurement, and therefore no border.

WR: In attention.

K: In complete attention.

WR: In that sense it is equal to awareness.

K: No.

WR: Why not?

K: In awareness there may be a center from which you are being aware.

SS: Even if there is no choice?

WR: No, that is not awareness.

K: Wait, I must go back.

GN: You are making a distinction between awareness and attention.

K: I want to.

SN: Are you saying attention is a deeper process?

K: Yes, much deeper, a totally different quality. One can be aware of what kind of dress you have. One may say "I like it" or "I don't like it," so choice doesn't exist, you are wearing it, that's all. But in attention there is no attender, one who attends, and so no division.

WR: You can also say the same thing of awareness, there is no one who is aware.

K: Of course, that's right. But it is not the same quality as attention.

WR: I don't want to go into these words, but the Buddha's teaching of *satipatthana* is that in this practice of meditation there is no discrimination, no value judgment, no like or dislike, you only see. That is all. And when you see, what happens will happen.

K: In that state of attention, what takes place?

WR: That needs another explanation.

K: No, if you totally attend, with your ears, your eyes, your body, your nerves, with all your mind and your heart in the sense of affection, love, compassion, with that total attention, what takes place?

WR: Of course what takes place is an absolute and complete internal revolution.

K: No, what is the state of such a mind that is completely attentive?

PM: It is free of the stream.

K: No, that is finished.

WR: The stream has dried up now, don't let's talk about it! It is now a desert!

K: I am asking what is the quality of the mind that is so supremely attentive?

PM: Compassionate?

K: You see it has no quality, no center, and having no center, it has no border. This is an actuality, you can't just imagine this. So has one ever given such complete attention to sorrow?

SS: Is there any object in that attention?

K: Of course not.

WR: Object in the sense of?

K: Subject and object. Obviously not, because there is no division. You try it, *do it*, sir.

SS: I mean not a merely physical object, but any phenomenal object such as sorrow, all those.

K: Give complete attention, if you can. Say for instance, I tell you meditation is the meditator.

WR: That is right, there is no meditator.

K: Wait, wait, wait! I say that meditation is the meditator. Give your complete attention to that, and see what happens. You don't make an abstraction of it into an idea, but you just hear that statement. It has a quality of truth, it has a quality of great beauty, there is a sense of absoluteness about it. Now give your whole attention to it and see what happens.

WR: I think Buddhist meditation, *satipatthana*, is that.

K: I don't know, sir. I'll accept your word for it, but I don't know.

WR: And I do not think that will be misleading because *satipatthana*, real *satipatthana*, is that. Now if you ask people who practice it, and there are so many meditation centers, I say frankly they are misleading. I have written about this.

K: Yes, sir, that is nonsense.

WR: When you ask how it happens, I said that presupposes a method, a technique.

K: No, I am asking: Can one give such attention?

WR: You are asking whether it is possible?

K: Yes, is it possible and will you give such attention? Not you, sir, I am just asking the question. Which means: do we ever attend?

PM: Sir, when you say: Can one attend . . .

K: Will you attend? Not exercising will.

PM: Quite.

K: Will you, you know, do it?

PM: Spontaneously, naturally, do it.

K: If that attention is not there, truth cannot exist.

WR: I don't think that is appropriate. Truth exists but cannot be seen.

K: Ah, I don't know. You say truth exists, but I don't know.

WR: But that doesn't mean that truth does not exist.

K: Jesus spoke of the Father in heaven, but I don't know the Father, he may exist but I don't know, so I don't accept that.

WR: Yes, it is right not to accept that, but I don't think it is correct to say that, without that attention, truth does not exist.

K: I said that without that attention truth cannot come into being.

WR: There is no coming into being.

K: No, of course not. All right, let me put it differently. Without that attention the word "truth" has no meaning.

WR: That is better.

K: We have talked for an hour and three quarters, sir, we had better stop.

WR: May I thank everyone.

Part Two

Why Don't We Change?

Expecting a Result

QUESTIONER: After having listened eagerly to you for so many years, we find ourselves exactly where we were. Is this all we can expect?

KRISHNAMURTI: The difficulty in this problem is that we want a result to convince ourselves that we have progressed, that we have been transformed. We want to know that we have arrived. And a man who has arrived, a man who has listened and got a result, has obviously not listened at all. [*laughter*] This is not a clever answer. The questioner says he has listened for many years. Now, has he listened with complete attention, or has he listened in order to arrive somewhere and be conscious of his arrival? It is like the man who practices humility. Can humility be practiced? Surely, to be conscious that you are humble is not to be humble. You want to know that you have arrived. This indicates—does it not?—that you are listening in order to achieve a particular state, a place where you will never be disturbed, where you will find everlasting happiness, permanent bliss.

But as I have said before, there is no arriving, there is only the movement of learning—and that is the beauty of life. If you have arrived, there is nothing more. And all of you have arrived, or you want to arrive, not only in your business, but also in everything you do; so you are dissatisfied, frustrated, and miserable. There is no place at which to arrive: there is just this movement of learning which becomes painful only when there is accumulation. A mind that listens with complete attention, will never look for a result, because it is constantly unfolding; like a river, it is always in movement. Such a mind is totally unconscious of its own activity, in the sense that there is no perpetuation of a self, of a "me" that is seeking to achieve an end.

The Lure of Enlightenment

The priests throughout the world, whether Christian, Buddhist, Hindu, or Tibetan, have always said that there is a promise of something greater. Do this and you will go to heaven, and if you don't you will go to hell. Which is interpreted in the Hindu version in one way, and in the others in another, but that is irrelevant. So our minds are conditioned heavily by something other than "what is." The other is the promised land, the never-never land, heaven, enlightenment, nirvana, the *moksha* of the Hindus. Because I don't know what to do with *this*, the "what is," my whole longing is for *that*.

It is put in different ways: the Communists want a perfect State, a perfect environment. It is the same problem, the same issue only put in different words—the tomorrow. So that may be—I am asking—one of the fundamental reasons why human beings don't change, because they have this—the perfect highest principle, called in India Brahman, or nirvana by the Buddhists, heaven by the Christians, and so on. That may be one of the fundamental reasons why human beings don't change. Or because of the perfect ideal, the perfect man or woman. Which means the "what is" is not important, but the perfect ideal is important, the perfect State is important, the nameless is important. So don't bother with "what is," don't look at "what is," but translate "what is" in terms of "what should be." You understand all this? I hope I am getting at you. So we have created a duality: the "what should be" and "what is." And we are saying that may be one of the major reasons why human beings don't change.

When there is this division between "what is" and "what should be," the highest, then there is conflict, right? Division between the Arab and the Jew. Wherever there is division there must be conflict, that is a law. So we have been conditioned in this division, to accept, to live in this division between the "what is" and "what should be." The "what should be" has been brought about because I don't know how to deal with "what is." Or the "what should be" is seen as a lever—you understand?—to get rid of "what is." So it is a conflict. So why has the mind created the "what should be"? And why is it not concerned totally with "what is"? Why has the mind done this? Why has thought done this?

Thought, if it is at all aware, knows it has created "what is," and thought says, "This is a fragment, this is transitory, that is permanent"—you understand? This "what is" is transitory, and thought has created the highest principle, which it thinks is permanent—thought thinks that. This is impermanent, that is permanent. Both being the creation of thought. Right? God, the Savior—all created by thought, the "what should be."

So thought has created this division, and then thought says, "I cannot solve this, but I am going to approach that." Now when you see the truth of *this*, *that* doesn't exist. Only *this* remains. I wonder if you see it? Thought has created the perfect ideal, the perfect State, perfect nirvana, perfect *moksha*, perfect heaven, because it does not know what to do with this, with "what is," with my sorrow, my agony, my impenetrable ignorance. So thought has created this division. Do you see the truth of it? Not verbal agreement, not acceptance, logical acceptance, but the truth of it? If you see the truth of it, then *that*—the ideal, the perfect—doesn't exist. Because you know nothing about it, it is merely a projection of thought. So then you have the energy to deal with "what is." Instead of losing energy out there, you have the energy to deal with what is happening. You see the difference? Oh, for God's sake! Do you see it? So you have the energy to deal with "what is."

Then you have to learn how to look at "what is." To observe "what is." Now you no longer have the duality created by "what should be," but only "what is." You are beginning to see the implications of it? When there is no "what should be," the highest principle, you have only this. This is a fact, and that is not a fact. So we can deal with facts. When there is no duality, there is only one thing, say, for instance, violence. There is only violence, not nonviolence. The nonviolence is "what should be." So when you see the truth of it, there is only violence, right? Now you have the energy to deal with that violence.

What is violence? Go into it with me for a moment. Violence: anger, competition, comparison, imitation—imitation being I am this, I must be that. So violence psychologically is comparison, imitation, various forms of conformity, essentially comparison—I am this, I must be that—that is violence. Not just throwing bombs, physical violence, that is something quite different. That is brought about by our rotten society, immoral society, we won't go into that.

So there is only this thing, violence. What is important there? What is the nature of it? We have described, more or less, what is violence. You may not agree with the description, but you know what we mean by violence—jealousy, anger, hatred, annoyance, arrogance, vanity, all that is part of the structure of violence. That violence comes with the picture, with the image I have, that is part of my image. Now can the mind be free of the image? As long as there is an image, a picture, I must be violent. The picture is formed through sensation, plus thought and the image—you are following this? So a human being realizes that as long as there is this image created through sensation plus thought, as long as that image—which is me—exists, I must be violent. Violence means "me" and "you," "we" and "they." So violence is there as long as this image exists. And that image is sensation plus thought. And there is no image if there is only complete sensation. So then we can deal with "what is." I wonder if you understand this?

Look: I am angry, or I hate somebody—I don't, but we will take that as an example. I hate somebody because he has done something ugly, hurt me and all the rest of it. My instinctual response, being a fairly intelligent, fairly normal human being, is to say, "I mustn't hate him, it is bad." I now have two images: I hate, and I mustn't hate. Two images. So there is a battle between these two images. One says: control, suppress, change, don't yield—you follow?—that goes on all the time as long as two images exist. And I know—I have realized this very deeply—that the images are formed through sensation plus thought. That is a fact. I have realized that. So I put away non-hate—you understand? I have only this feeling of annoyance, anger, hatred. What is that feeling, created through the image, by some action of another? You have done something to the image that is me. And that image is hurt, and the reaction to that hurt is anger. And if I have no image, thought, sensation, if I have no image, you don't touch me—you understand? There is no wounding, there is no hate—which is "what is." Now I know, I am aware of what to do with the "what is." Have you got something of this?

So I have found human beings don't change because they are wasting their energy, don't change because they are exercising their will, which they think is extraordinarily noble, which is called freedom of choice. And also they don't know what to do with "what is" and therefore project "what should be," and also perhaps because *that*, nirvana, *moksha*, heaven, is far more important than "what is." These are the blocks that prevent human beings from changing, this is why they don't radically transform themselves. If you have understood this deeply, with your blood, with your heart, with all your senses, then you will see that there is an extraordinary transformation without the least effort.

Seeing One's Conditioning

Can we, as human beings living in this terrible world that we have created, bring about a radical change in ourselves? That is the whole point. Some philosophers and others have said that human conditioning is impossible to change radically; you can modify, polish, and refine it, but the basic quality of conditioning you cannot alter. There are a great many people who think that—the existentialists and so on. Why do we accept such conditioning? You are following, I hope, what we are talking about. Why do we accept our conditioning, which has brought about this really mad, insane world? Where we want peace and are supplying armaments, where we want peace and are nationalistically, economically, socially dividing each other, where we want peace and all religions, their organizations, are making us separate, as they are. There is such vast contradiction out there as well as in ourselves. I wonder if one is aware of all this in ourselves, not what is happening out there. Most of us know what is happening out there, you don't have to be very clever to find out, you just observe. And the confusion out there is partly responsible for our own conditioning. We are asking: Is it possible to bring about in ourselves a radical transformation of this? Because only then can we have a good society, where we won't hurt each other psychologically as well as physically.

When we ask this question of ourselves, what is our deep response? One is conditioned, not only as an Englishman, a German or Frenchman, and so on, but also one is conditioned by various forms of desire, belief, pleasure and conflict, and also by psychological conflict. All that and more contributes to this conditioning.

We will go into it. We are asking ourselves—thinking together, as I hope we are—can this conditioning, this human prison with its grief, loneliness, anxiety, personal assertions, demands, fulfillment, and all that—that is our conditioning, our consciousness, and our consciousness is its content—can that whole structure be transformed? Otherwise we will never have peace in this world. There will perhaps be small modifications but man will be fighting, quarrelling, perpetually in conflict within himself and outwardly. So that is our question. Can we think together about this?

Then the question arises: What is one to do? One is aware that one is conditioned, knows, is conscious of it. This conditioning has come into being from one's own desires, self-centered activities, through lack of right relationship with each other, one's own sense of loneliness. One may live among a great many people, may have intimate relationships, but there is always this sense of empty whirl within oneself. All that is our conditioning, intellectual, psychological, emotional, and also of course physical. Now can this be totally transformed? That, I feel, is the real revolution. One in which there is no violence.

Now, can we do this together? Or if you do it, if you understand the conditioning and resolve that conditioning, and another is conditioned, will the one who is conditioned listen to another? Perhaps you are unconditioned. Will I listen to you? And what will make me listen? What pressure, what influence, what reward? What will make me listen to you with my heart, my mind, my whole being? Because if one can listen so completely, perhaps the solution is there. But apparently we don't seem to listen. So we are asking: What will make a human being, knowing his conditioning—and most of us do if we are at all intelligently aware—what will make him change? Please put this question to yourself, find out what will make each one of us bring about a change, a freedom from this conditioning. Not to jump into another conditioning.

That is like leaving Catholicism and becoming a Buddhist, it is the same pattern.

So what will make each one of us—who all, surely, want to bring about a good society—change? Change has been promised through reward—heaven, a new kind of carrot, a new ideology, a new community, a new set of groups, new gurus. Or a punishment—"If you don't do this you will go to hell." So our whole thinking is based on this principle of reward and punishment. "I will do this if I can get something out of it." But that kind of attitude, or that way of thinking, doesn't bring about radical change. And such a change is absolutely necessary. I am sure we are all aware of it. So what shall we do?

Some of you have listened to the speaker for a number of years—I wonder why? And having listened, it becomes a new kind of "mantra." Do you know what that word means? It is a Sanskrit word whose true meaning is not to be self-centered, and to ponder over not becoming. That is its meaning. Abolish self-centeredness, and ponder, meditate, look at yourself, so that you don't become something. The real meaning of that word has been ruined by all the transcendental meditation nonsense.

So some of you have listened for many years. And do we listen and therefore bring about a change, or have we got used to the words and just carry on? What will make a human being who has lived for so many million years, carrying on the same old pattern, inheriting the same instincts, self-preservation, fear, security, sense of self-concern which brings about great isolation, what will make him change? A new god, a new form of entertainment, a new religious football, a new kind of circus with all that stuff? What will make us change? Sorrow has apparently not changed man, because we have suffered a great deal, not only individually but collectively. As humankind we have suffered an enormous amount—wars, disease, pain, death. We have suffered enormously, and apparently sorrow has not changed us. Neither has fear changed us, because our mind is constantly pursuing, seeking out pleasure, and even that pleasure is the same pleasure in different forms, and hasn't changed us. So what will make us change?

We don't seem to be able to do anything voluntarily. We will do things under pressure. If there was no pressure, no sense of reward or punishment—but reward and punishment are too silly to even think about! If there was no sense of the future—I don't know if you have gone into that whole question of the future, that may be where we deceive ourselves psychologically—we will go into that presently. If you abandon all those, then what is the quality of the mind that faces absolutely the present? Do you understand my question? Are we communicating with each other? Please, say yes or no, I don't know where we are. I hope I'm not talking to myself!

Does one realize that one is in a prison created by oneself? Oneself being the result of the past, parents, grandparents and so on—the inherited, acquired, imposed psychological prison in which we live. And naturally the instinct is to break out of that prison. Now does one realize that, not as an idea, not as a concept, but as an actuality, as psychologically a fact? When one faces that fact, why is it that even then there is no possibility of change? You understand my question?

This has been a problem for all serious people who are concerned with the human tragedy, human misery, and who ask themselves why don't we all bring about a sense of clarity in ourselves, a sense of freedom, a sense of being essentially good? I don't know if you have noticed that the intellectuals, the literary people, the writers and the so-called world leaders, have given up talking about bringing about a good society. We were talking the other day to some of these people, and they said, "What nonsense that is, that is old-fashioned, throw it out. There is no such thing as a good society any more. That is Victorian, stupid, nonsensical. We have to accept things as they are and live with them." And probably for most of us it is like that. So you and I, as two friends, talking over this, what shall we do?

The authority of another doesn't bring about this change, right? If I accept you as my authority because I want to bring about a revolution in myself, and so perhaps bring about a good society, the very idea of my following you, you instructing me, that ends good society. I wonder if you see that? I am not good because you tell me to be good, or because I accept you as the supreme authority on righteousness and I follow you. The very acceptance of authority and obedience is the very destruction of a good society. Isn't that so? I wonder if you see this? May we go further into it?

If I have a guru—thank God, I haven't—if I have a guru and I follow him, what have I done to myself? What have I done in the world? Nothing. He tells me some nonsense about how to meditate, this or that, and I will have a marvelous experience or levitate, all the rest of that nonsense, and my intention is to bring about a good society, where we can be happy, where there is a sense of affection, a relationship where there is no barrier, that is what I long for. I go to you as my guru and what have I done? I have destroyed the very thing that I wanted, because apart from the authority of law and so forth, psychological authority is divisive, is in its very nature separative. You up there and I down below, and so you are always progressing higher and higher, and I am also progressing higher and higher, and we never meet! [*laughter*] You laugh, I know, but this is actually what we are doing.

So can I realize that authority, with its implication of organization, will never free me? Authority gives one a sense of security. "I don't know, I am confused, but *you* know, or at least I *think* you know, that's good enough for me, I invest my energy and my demand for security in you, in what you are talking about." And we create an organization around that and that very organization becomes the prison. I don't know if you know all this? That's why one should not belong to any spiritual organization, however

promising, however enticing, however romantic. Can we even accept, see that together? You understand my question? See it together to be a fact and therefore when we see that together it is
finished. See that the very nature of authority and obedience with
its organization, religious and otherwise, is separative, setting up a
hierarchical system, which is what is happening in the world, and
is therefore part of the destructive nature of the world, see the
truth of that and throw it out. Can we do that? So that none of
us—sorry—so that none of us belong to any spiritual organizations, that means religious organizations, Catholic, Protestant,
Hindu, Buddhist, none of them.

By belonging to something we feel secure, obviously. But belonging to something invariably brings about insecurity because in
itself it is separative. You have your guru, your authority, you are a
Catholic, Protestant, and somebody else is something else. So they
never meet, though all organized religions say that they are all
working together for truth. So can we, listening to each other, to
this fact, banish from our thinking all sense of acceptance of authority, psychological authority, and therefore all the organizations created around it? Then what happens? Have I dropped
authority because you have said so, or because I see the destructive
nature of these so-called organizations? And do I see it as fact and
therefore with intelligence? Or just vaguely accept it? I don't know
if you are following this? If one sees the fact, the very perception
of that fact is intelligence, and in that intelligence there is security, not in some superstitious nonsense. I wonder if you see? Would
you tell me, are we meeting each other?

AUDIENCE: Yes.

K: No, not verbally, please. That is very easy because we are all
speaking English or French or whatever it is. Intellectually, verbally is not meeting together. It is when you see the fact together.

Now can we—we are asking—can we look at the fact of our

conditioning? Not the idea of our conditioning. The fact that we are British, German, American, Russian, or Hindu, Eastern or whatever it is, that is one thing. Physical conditioning, brought about through economic reasons, climate, food, clothes and so on. But also there is a great deal of psychological conditioning. Can we look at that as fact? Like fear. Can you look at that? Or if you can't for the moment, can we look at the hurts that we have received, the wounds, the psychological wounds that we have treasured, have received from childhood. Look at it, not analyze it. The psychotherapists go back and investigate the past. That is, they seek the cause of the wounds that one has received, investigating and analyzing the whole movement of the past. That is generally called analysis in psychotherapy. Now discovering the cause, does that help? And you have taken a lot of time, years perhaps, it is a game that we all play because we never want to face the fact but say instead, "Let's investigate how the facts have come into being." I don't know if you are following all this?

So you are expending a great deal of energy, and probably a great deal of money, on professional investigation into the past; or on your own investigation, if you are capable of it. And we are saying such forms of analysis are separative because the analyzer thinks he is different from the thing he is analyzing. You are following all this? So he maintains this division through analysis, whereas the obvious fact is the analyzer is the analyzed. I wonder if you see that? The moment one recognizes that the analyzer is the analyzed—because when you are angry you are that—the observer *is* the observed. When there is the actual reality of that, then analysis has no meaning, there is only pure observation of the fact which is happening now. I wonder if you see this? It may be rather difficult, because most of us are so conditioned to the analytical process, self-examination, introspective investigation, we are so accustomed to that, so conditioned by it, that perhaps if something new is said you instantly reject it or you withdraw. So please investigate, look at it.

We are asking: Is it possible to look at the fact as it is happening now—anger, jealousy, violence, pleasure, fear, whatever it is—to look at it, not analyze it, just to look at it, and in that very observation is the observer merely observing the fact as something separate from himself, or is he the fact? I wonder if you get this? Am I making myself clear? You understand the distinction? Most of us are conditioned to the idea that the observer is different from the thing observed. I have been greedy. Or I have been violent. At the moment of violence there is no division, it is only later on that thought picks it up and separates itself from the fact. So the observer is the past looking at what is actually happening now. So can you look at the fact, that you are angry, miserable, lonely, whatever it is, look at that fact without the observer saying, "I am separate" and looking at it differently. Or does he recognize the fact *is* himself, there is no division between the fact and himself? The fact is himself. I wonder if you see.

And what therefore happens when that actuality takes place? Look, my mind has been conditioned to look at the fact, which is loneliness, let us take that—no, we began with being hurt from childhood, let's look at that. I have been accustomed, used to thinking that I am different from the hurt, right? And therefore my action toward that hurt is either suppression and avoidance or building around my hurt a resistance so that I don't get hurt any more. Therefore that hurt is making me more and more isolated, more and more afraid. So this division has taken place because I think I am different from the hurt. Are you following all this? But the hurt is me. The "me" is the image that I have created about myself, which is hurt, right?

So I have created an image through education, my family, society, through all the religious ideas of soul, separativeness, the individual, all that. I have created an image about myself, and when you tread on that image, I get wounded. Then I say that hurt is not me, I must do something about that hurt. So I maintain the division between the hurt and myself. But the fact is the image is me which has been hurt. Right? So can I look at that fact? Look at the fact that the image is myself and as long as I have the image about myself somebody is going to tread on it. That's a fact. Can the mind be free of that image? Because one realizes that as long as that image exists you are going to do something to it, put a pin into it, and therefore there will be hurt, with the result of isolation, fear, resistance, building a wall around myself—all that takes place when there is the division between the observer and the observed, which is the hurt. This is not intellectual, please. This is just ordinary observing oneself, which we referred to at the beginning as "self-awareness."

So what takes place when the observer is the observed—the actuality of it, not the idea of it—what takes place? I have been hurt from childhood, through school, through parents, other boys and girls, you know, I have been hurt, wounded, psychologically. And I carry that hurt throughout my life, hidden, anxious, frightened, and I know the result of all that. And now I see that as long as the image which I have created, which has been put together, as long as that exists, there will be hurt. That image is me. Can I look at that fact? Not looking at it as an idea, but looking at the actual fact that the image is hurt, the image is me. I wonder if you see? Could we come together, think together, on that one point at least?

Then what takes place? Previously, the observer tried to do something about it. Here the observer is absent. Therefore he can't do anything about it. You get it? You understand what has taken place? Previously the observer exerted himself in suppressing it, controlling it, not to be hurt, isolating himself, resisting and all the rest of it, making a tremendous effort. But when the fact is seen that the observer is the observed, then what takes place? Do you want me to tell you? Then we are nowhere, then what I tell you will have no meaning. But if we have come together, think together and come to this point, then you will discover for yourself that as long as you make an effort there is the division, right? So in pure observation there is no effort, and therefore the thing that has been put together as image begins to dissolve. That is the whole point.

Disorder and the Heart

It seems to me that one of our great problems is order and disorder, freedom and conformity. Until we resolve this question within ourselves, not as a group, not as a community or by organized acceptance of a certain formula—unless we, as human beings, as individuals, resolve this problem, our revolt or freedom will only be a further process of confusion and conflict. We conform—that is fairly obvious—right through the world, hoping that conformity will bring about order. We must have order. No society, no individual—within or without—can have disorder; there must be order. And order is not possible by merely stating what order is, in terms of a categorical or a patterned order.

Order, it seems to me, can only come about when we discover for ourselves what breeds disorder. Out of the understanding of what brings about disorder naturally will come order. That is fairly simple. When I know what brings about disorder in a family, in myself, or in society, and if I wish, as a human being, to bring about order, I must first clarify or put away disorder. So, the order of which we are talking is not a positive act, but rather it comes about through the understanding of the negation of what is disorder. If I understand what is disorder and negate it, put it aside, clarify, inquire into all the implications involved, if I understand the totality of disorder, this may appear superficially as negation. But out of this understanding of disorder comes a natural order: not the other way round, not conforming to what is considered as order—such conformity only breeds greater disorder. We are human beings in conflict, in fear, in anxiety, with a great many problems of obedience, acceptance, anxiety, seeking power, and so on. And so merely to seek order, or the pattern of order, and then conform to that pattern essentially breeds disorder.

Please, we must understand this, not verbally. Because, you know, it is one of the most unfortunate things that we all preach endlessly, write books, have theories, formulas and concepts, and there is no action at all. We are masters, especially in this unfortunate country, at verbalizing, theorizing, having concepts, formulas, and exploring these concepts dialectically, hoping that, through the discovery of the truth in theories, we will come to action; and therefore there is inaction, we do not do a thing. So we must at the very beginning understand that order cannot possibly be brought about through conformity to a pattern, under any circumstances—whether it is a Communist order or a religious order or a personal demand for orderliness. This order, which is extraordinarily positive, can only come about through understanding this issue very profoundly, because we are going to go into things with which you will presently not agree at all—at least I hope you will neither accept nor discard; that leads nowhere.

So we have to find out what causes disorder in the world outside and within. The understanding of the disorder outwardly brings about the understanding of the disorder inwardly. But this disorder, which we divide as the outer and the inner, is essentially one and the same; they are not two separate disorders, because each of us, as a human being, is both society and the individual. The individual is not separate from society; the individual has created the psychological structure of society, and in that psychological structure he is caught. And therefore he tries to break away from that psychological structure, which is a mere revolt and therefore does not resolve any problem.

We have to inquire into what creates disorder, because out of disorder nothing can grow, nothing can function. You must have tremendous order to bring about the understanding of truth, or whatever one likes to call it. You must have great order, and this order cannot possibly come about through revolt, or through conformity, or through acceptance of a formula—socialist, capitalist, religious, or any other formula.

So what brings about disorder? You understand? There must be order in the world. There is no order now in the world. War is the essence of disorder, whether it is in Vietnam or here or in Europe; war at any level, for any cause, is disorder. And why is there this disorder in the world—in this world in which we have to live and function as human beings? We are going to examine that; we are not examining it verbally or theoretically or statistically, but actually, factually. When you understand the fact, then you say that you prefer either to go that way or not to go that way.

So what brings disorder in the world, psychologically, inwardly? Obviously, one of the reasons of this enormous, destructive disorder in the world is the division of religions: you a Hindu and I a Muslim; you a Christian—Catholic, Protestant, Episcopalian—a multitude of divisions. Obviously religion has been put together by man in order to help him to become civilized, not to seek God—you cannot find God through beliefs, dogmas, through rituals, through repetition, through reading the *Gita* or the Bible, or through following a priest. This world is divided into religions—organized religions with their dogmas, with their rituals, with their beliefs, with their superstitions, throughout the world. And religions do not bring people together at all. They talk about it, they say, "If you see God, we are all brothers." But we are not brothers! We are looking at facts and not at hopes and theories.

So religions have separated man, and that is one of the factors of great disorder. You are not agreeing with me, you see the facts. You see how, in Christendom, for two thousand years they have been fighting each other, Catholics and Protestants, Catholics among themselves, and there have been tortures. And this has happened in this country—the Muslims against the Hindus and the Hindus against the Muslims; one guru against another guru; one guru having fewer disciples, the other having more and wanting more!

Please do listen to all this, because we are reaching a great crisis in our lives, not only as individuals but as a community. And any man who wants not only to bring about order in himself, but to bring about a good society—not a great society, but a good society—needs to resolve this problem. So, we can see factually in the world that religions have separated man and that there have been tremendous, religious wars in the East as well as in the West. So that is one of the roots of disorder. The organized beliefs with their churches, rituals, have become a tremendous corporation, a business affair, which has nothing to do with religion.

And nationalism, a recent poisonous growth, is also the cause of disorder. This country probably has never been nationalistic. Europe has divided itself into many sovereign states, fighting each other, and tearing at each other for more land, for greater economic expansion and so on. They have had recently two tremendous, destructive wars within the memory of man. Nationalism has divided the people—the Englishman, the Frenchman, the Indian. And now you are becoming nationalistic in this country also. It is hoped that, through nationalism, human beings can be united. Worshiping the same flag, a piece of cloth—that has no meaning. [*laughter*] Please do not laugh. This is not a rhetorical or amusing, entertaining gathering. We are very serious, we are concerned with immense problems.

War has brought disorder in the world. War is always destructive, there is never a righteous war. And there have been within the recorded history of mankind, I believe, something like 14,600 wars and more. Since 1945 there have been forty wars! In the first war, the people might have said, "Let us hope this will be the last war!" The mothers, wives, husbands, children, must have cried. And we are still crying, after these 5,500 years. People have accepted war as the way of life. Here in India you are also accepting war as the way of life: more armaments, more generals, more soldiers. And as long as you have sovereign governments—that is, nationalistic separate governments, sovereign governments with their armies—you are bound to have wars. You may not have your son killed at Banaras, but you will have a son killed in Vietnam, whether he is an American or a Vietnamese. So, as long as there are sovereign governments, there must be war.

And what is a man to do who says, "I will not kill"? You understand? In this country, for generations upon generations, a certain class of people has been brought up not to kill, not to hurt an animal, a fly. And all that is gone. They will write volumes about the spiritual inheritance of India, but the actual fact is that we have destroyed all that inheritance; we are just verbally repeating something which is not real.

So we have two issues involved: What is a human being to do in a country like this, or in Europe, or in America, when he asserts he will not kill? And strangely, in this country for several years, perhaps thirty years or so, you have been preaching nonviolence— you have been shouting it from the housetops; that has been the export from this country to the West —"Don't kill," "*Ahimsa*," and so on. Now you are brought together, united by war! Somebody told me yesterday with great enthusiasm, with great pleasure, that war has united India as never before! I have been told this in several places, by several people. You know, this is not very strange. This has happened in England, where class division is as strong as here; they all slept together in the underground, they were all terribly united through hate! And you have the spurious arguments: What will you do, if you are in the government; would you not fight if you were attacked? Obviously, if you are in a government, if you are the head of a sovereign state with an army, with all the paraphernalia of uncivilized existence, you are bound to attack or to defend. Nowadays nobody talks about being attacked or defending. You are at war; do not justify war!

Please, sirs, listen to all this, it is your life. We people have gone, we are going. In this country, in spite of its nonviolence, its preaching of non-killing for thousands upon thousands of years, there has not been one human being who has said, "We will not kill." There have been whispering campaigns; you and I privately tell each other in our rooms that we won't kill. But publicly we never get on a platform and say, "I won't kill," and go to prison or get shot for saying it. There has not been one boy or girl or one human being who has stood up against the stream. When it was popular to preach nonviolence we all supported it. Now that war is popular, you also go for it. I am not talking of such individuals.

What is a human being to do who says that he will not kill? What is he to do? He cannot do anything, can he? Either he can go to prison, or be shot, killed by the government, because he is a rebel, disloyal—you know all the words put out by the politicians and by the religio-political entities. Please inquire into yourselves: why is it that there has not been one human being in India who said, "This is wrong, killing is wrong"? Not as governments, but as a human being, why is it that you have not said it? Must you be challenged? Through all the various organizations created for nonviolence, why have they not stood up? There is something very radically wrong in this country, when they have not got that conviction of what they believe. So nationalism is disorder, it breeds disorder. War breeds disorder. Obviously, religions also breed disorder. So civilized man, a man who is really human, will not accept sovereign governments. You understand? You say, "I am a Hindu"—who cares whether you are a Hindu, a Chinese, or whatever you call yourself? What matters is what you are, not what your labels are.

So unless you, as a human being, are free from all these labels—

Socialist, Communist, Capitalist, American, Englishman, Indian, Muslim—as long as you are labeling yourself in any way, secretly or openly, you are breeding disorder in the world. And also you are breeding disorder outside and inside, when you belong to any religious group, or follow any guru. Because truth is not to be found by following somebody, by making it all easy for you as a pattern: doing this, following this, meditating this way, disciplining this way. You will never get it that way. To find truth you must be free. You must stand alone, swim against the current, battle. You know, I was told the other day that this war that India has had, is justified because the *Bhagavad-Gita* said so! I thought that was rather lovely—don't you?

So what are you going to do about it—not as Indians? What are you, as a human being, confronted with this problem—what are you going to do about it? There is poverty in this country, tremendous poverty—you know it as well as I do. And this poverty is going to increase because of this war. There is lack of rain, also inefficiency, corruption, and national divisions. We will accept food from one country and not from another—all politics! So, as a human being, what are you going to do? Either you accept disorder and continue to live in disorder and therefore inefficiency and therefore wars, therefore poverty, therefore hunger, or, as a human being, you reject it totally, not partially. You cannot reject something partially, you do not reject poison a little bit, you reject the whole thing. And that means you have to stand alone. Then you will be despised by society. You will be shot. Probably not in this country, it is not too efficient yet. In Europe, during the last world war, many were killed. A mother we know had a son, a boy of eighteen—not a grown-up like you—who refused to go to kill, and he was shot. That boy did not talk about nonviolence, ahimsa, the *Gita*, non-killing, none of that. He did not want to kill, and he was killed.

So seeing all this, the outer disorder and inward disorder, merely to become a pacifist is not the answer. The answer is much deeper than all this. But to find the answer, one has to reject the obvious things. You cannot keep the obvious things that are poisoning you, and then try to see much deeper. You cannot say, "I will have my pet guru and follow him, accept what he says and meditate, and then try to seek a much deeper answer." The two cannot go together. Either you reject the total thing, or not at all—reject as human beings but not as a collective body. Because, when you become a collective body and reject, then you are merely conforming and you may have the support of a hundred or a million people behind you—that is a mere following of another, in a different way. But to stand out completely alone—that is a very difficult thing for most people, because they are frightened of losing their job. You know all this.

So seeing all this enormous disorder in ourselves and in the world, how is one to bring about any order? As we said, order will come when we understand disorder, when we cease to be nationalist, when we are really seeking truth, freedom—not through some organization, not through some belief, not through some guru.

Now, what makes each one of us change—you understand? That is the real question. What makes you, who have been nationalistic, or a tremendously devout person with regard to some guru, change? To me the word "guru" is poison, and there is something ugly in human beings following anybody. Now, how will you drop all this? How will you drop your Hinduism, your gurus, your nationalism? How will you stand alone, not follow what everybody says? What will make us, as human beings, do this? That is the real issue. You understand, sirs? What will make you divest all this at one blow, one breath, and say, "I am out"? Probably, most of you have not thought of all this at all. You have never said to yourself in your heart, "Why have I not stood up with tears in my eyes not to kill anybody?" Why have you not done it? Don't invent reasons. Why have you not done it?

And what will make you change? That is the real issue. Either you say, "I do not want to change, I will accept things as they are. That is good enough for me; there is disorder, poverty, there is starvation; there will be wars. There have been wars for five thousand years and more, and we will have some more wars. What does it matter? The world is maya anyhow, and what does it all matter?" You accept it, as most of you apparently do. Because we human beings have an extraordinary capacity to adjust to anything—to living in a small room for the sake of God, doubled up, having one meal, a tortured mind; or to the appalling, bestial conditions of war, not at Banaras but at the front, in Vietnam, whether American or Vietnamese. Human beings can adjust themselves to anything, to dirt and squalor in the streets, open gutters, a corrupt municipality; they can put up with anything. After all, adjustability is the difference between animals and human beings—animals cannot adjust, but human beings can.

So either we accept things as they are and go along miserably, torturing ourselves, unhappy, killing and being killed, seeking fulfillment and being frustrated, wanting to be leaders, restless, unhappy—which is what we are doing. If you accept that, there is nothing more to be said. You understand? You say, "That is my life, that is the way my father lived, my grandfather lived, my sons will live. And generations will come that will live likewise." If you accept that, that is all right. Don't introduce another problem. If you don't accept it, as a man of affection who feels strongly, who feels this whole monstrous thing, then what are you to do? How is such a man to change? How is he to bring about a mutation within himself? And that mutation perhaps will not, or will, affect society—but that is irrelevant. Society wants this disorder—not wars; but greed, envy, competition, seeking for power, position. That is what society is. And when you see all that, how will you change? You understand my question, sirs? How will you change?

May I proceed to point out what brings about this enormous

mutation in a human mind? May I go on with it? Wait, sirs. I will go on. But it is not a verbal statement, it is not a thing about which you say, "I agree" or "I disagree." Because if you see there is disorder, and you are passionate, you do not say, "Show me the way and I will follow it." We are not talking of like and dislike, what is convenient, what is not convenient, nor in terms of a Communist, a Socialist, a Hindu, a Buddhist, or whatever you are. We are talking nonverbally, factually, about the necessity of tremendous, human change. Because, you see, the electronic brains, automation, and other technological things are going to bring about a certain change in the world. Man is going to have more leisure—it is not yet in this country; it is coming in Europe, and the beginning of it is already in America. So all these things, automation, computers, wars, nationalism, these religious differences—to face all these and to break through all these, there must be in each one of us, not as a collective group belonging to some organization, but as human beings, a tremendous mutation. How will you change? What is the thing, what is the element, what is the energy that is necessary to break down this tremendous destructive chaos in which one lives?

What makes one change, even a little bit? Say, for instance, you smoke, if you do. What will make you drop it? Doctors state that your lungs will be affected, and that is one of the ways of making you drop smoking—through fear. Punishment and reward—those are the only things that will force us to change. Punishment and reward; heaven and hell; next life and therefore behave in this life; therefore the carrot and the whip—that is, punishment and reward. That is the only thing we know: "It gives me greater profit, greater satisfaction, greater energy, greater amusement, greater excitement, greater adventure; therefore I will do it!" Now, any change taking place through punishment and reward—is that change? Please, sirs, you have to answer this question, not I. So don't go to sleep! Is that a radical change, not a superficial change?

Superficial change—we have done that for centuries, and that has not brought any mutation in the human being, any revolution in the human mind. We are asking the question much more fundamentally.

If there is no punishment and reward, what will make you change? And there is no punishment and reward. Who is going to punish you, who is going to reward you? All those things are over. God is not going to reward you for righteous behavior; he does not care two pins for your behavior, right or wrong. The Church no longer has any importance. You may go to "confession" and so on, in Europe that is Catholic. But all that is disappearing, all that is being thrown overboard, except in the most backward states. Perhaps in India, where you say a little but not too much, you pretend to be a little more careful; that is all. But actually there is nobody to punish and reward. On the contrary, society says, "Come along; be greedy, be envious, be competitive, fight, quarrel; kill the Muslim and the Muslim will kill you." Society loves that, and the politicians play up to it! So there is nobody who is going to reward you or punish you—nobody. Neither your guru—you don't believe in gurus anyhow—nor your gods and goddesses will reward or punish you. Probably your wife or husband can only punish you. When you have a family, your wife says, "I am not going to sleep with you tonight" or "I am not going to do this or that"—that is all!

So as there is no reward and no punishment—and there is not any actually, when you investigate—how will you bring about this change? You understand the problem that is getting more and more complex for each one of us? Is this a problem to you? It must be, if you are at all thoughtful, serious, if you have watched the world's events. Seeing what is taking place in this country; knowing that religions have no meaning any more—probably they never had it—seeing the futility of sacred books; seeing the absurdity of following any guru, however profitable, however pleasant; seeing that nobody can give you freedom, nobody can give you a mind that is healthy, strong, and deeply silent; seeing that no society, nobody is going to punish you or reward you—seeing all this and realizing that human beings must change radically, fundamentally, deep down, how will this change come about?

Shall we stop there this morning? Let us stop here this morning and continue on the morning of the twenty-fifth. You will perhaps be good enough—I am not asking you or trying to persuade you—to ask questions or discuss what we have been talking about.

Q: I see all that you have said this morning. But there is no change.

K: Let us go slowly and clearly, without any sentimentality involved in it.

Q: I am not sentimental. I see clearly.

K: I want to clarify your question to myself. There are two ways of looking at things. Either one sees intellectually, verbally, all that we have been talking about. Verbally, that is superficially. Then the question, "How am I to change?" will never occur to that person. He will say, "It has been like this and it will go on like this." Or he says, "I see it, I smell it, I taste it, it boils within me; I am burning with it, and yet action does not come out." And there is the other who sees it and the very act of seeing is the act.

Q: Sir, this has not happened at all, though you have talked about it for forty years.

K: We know very well, perhaps just as you do, that for forty years we have talked about all this, and many of you here have listened to me for forty years. And you go your way and we go our way. We are not discouraged, nor are you! Basically you are not discouraged; you want that way, you go that way.

And the gentleman says, "You have talked for forty years and what a waste of time!" I do not feel it that way at all. We have other problems.

Q: You have isolated yourself from the world altogether, and therefore you are happy.

K: Why don't you do the same?

Q: We are all ordinary human beings.

K: We cannot afford to be ordinary human beings any more. It was all right at one time. You cannot afford to be an ordinary, mediocre, dull, stupid, human being any more. The challenge is too immense. You will have to do something. So let us go through this slowly, sir. If you see it intellectually, there is no problem to you. If you see this whole thing from a comfortable easy chair—of course you happen to have a little money or a good job or . . .

Q: Let us have it out, Sir.

K: I am glad we know each other, we can fight it out. And if you belong to some Socialist organization, Communist or whatever it is, then you want the world to change according to that pattern, because you play an important part or you are a leader, you are this, and it gives you a certain importance—you all love that. That is one kind of person. Then there is the other kind—intellectuals who talk, who preach, who write books, who go to meetings, who cannot be kept away from any meetings, who always want to talk, talk. Then there are the others who see this mess, this confusion, this disorder, this misery, this agony that is going on in the world, and don't know what to do. They cannot break away from their nationalism, from their religion, from their gurus, and so on and on.

Then there are very few who say, "Look, I see this chaos, actual chaos"; and the very perception of it is action—not that they see it and act later. It is like seeing something poisonous and dropping it. There are very few of this kind, because that demands tremendous energy, inquiry, application, attention, stripping yourself of all your vanity, of all your stupidity, of everything.

The intellectual obviously will have his own kind of armchair; he takes away this armchair, but he will invent another armchair. If you take away this organization, he becomes a super-Communist or something else. So, there is only the middleman left, who says, "I see it, I do not know what to do, tell me what to do. Tell me the next step; step by step tell me, and I will follow it." That is his difficulty. He is looking for somebody else to tell him what to do. Instead of following the old bearded gentlemen and ladies who have been your gurus, you throw them away and you come to me and say, "You are my guru, please tell me what to do." And I refuse to be put in that position.

Q: Still the question remains: Why in spite of your talking about this for forty years, not a single human being has become different?

K: The gentleman asks why is it that though I have talked for forty years more or less of the same thing in different words and expressing it differently, there has not been one human being who is different? Why? Will you answer it, sir? Either what is being said is false and therefore has no position in the world; it is false and has no validity, and therefore you do not pay attention; your own reason, your own intelligence, your own affection, your own good sense says, "What rubbish you are talking!" Or you hear what is being said, but it means nothing to you, because the other is much more important.

Q: Why should truth be so impotent?

K: Because truth has no action. Truth is weak. Truth is not utilitarian, truth cannot be organized. It is like the wind, you cannot catch it, you cannot take hold of it in your fist and say, "I have caught it." Therefore it is tremendously vulnerable, impotent like the blade of grass on the roadside—you can kill it, you can destroy it. But we want it as a thing to be used for a better structure of society. And I am afraid you cannot use it, you cannot—it is like love, love is never potent. It is there for you, take it or leave it.

So, sirs, the problem is not that we have spoken for forty years. But the problem is: How is a human being, who has listened for forty years with a dry heart, without a tear in his eyes, who sees all this and does not do a thing, whose heart is broken up, whose heart is empty, whose mind is full of words and theories, and full of himself—how is he to make his heart love again? That is the real question.

The Negation of "What Is"

There were four or five people in the room. Some were students, others college graduates with jobs. One of the students said:

"I listened to you last year, and again this year. I know we are all conditioned. I am aware of society's brutalities, and of my own envy and anger. I know also the history of the Church and its wars and its unprincipled activities. I have studied history and the endless wars of the entrenched beliefs and ideologies that are creating so much conflict in the world. This mania of man—which is me also—seems to hold us and we seem to be doomed forever, unless, of course, we can bring about a change in ourselves. It's the small minority that really matters, that really having changed itself can do something in this murderous world. And a few of us have come, representing others, to discuss this matter with you. I think some of us are serious, and I don't know how far this seriousness will carry us. So first of all, taking us as we are, half-serious, somewhat hysterical, unreasonable, carried away by our assumptions and vanities—taking us as we are, can we really change? If not, we're going to destroy each other; our own species will disappear. There may be reconciliation in all this terror but there is always the danger of some maniacal group letting loose the atom bomb, and then we shall all be engulfed in it. So seeing all this, which is fairly obvious, which is being described endlessly by authors, professors, sociologists, politicians and so on—is it possible to change radically?"

KRISHNAMURTI: Some of us are not quite sure that we want to change, for we enjoy this violence. For some of us it is even profitable. And for others, all they desire is to remain in their entrenched positions. There are still others who through change seek some form of superexcitement, overrated emotional expression. Most of us want power in some form or another. The power over oneself, the power over another, the power that comes with new and brilliant ideas, the power of leadership, fame, and so on. Political power is as evil as religious power. The power of the world and the power of an ideology do not change man. Nor does the volition to change, the will to transform oneself, bring about this change.

"I can understand that," said the student. "Then what is the way of change if will, if principles and ideologies are not the way? Then what is the motive power? And change—to what?"

The older people in the room listened to this rather seriously. They were all attentive, and not one of them looked out of the window to see the green-yellow bird sitting on a branch sunning himself that early morning, preening himself, grooming his feathers and looking at the world from the height of that tall tree.

One of the older men said, "I am not at all sure that I want any change at all. It might be for the worse. It's better, this orderly disorder, than an order which may mean uncertainty, total insecurity and chaos. So when you talk of how to change, and the necessity of change, I am not at all sure I agree with you, my friend. As a speculative idea I enjoy it. But a revolution which will deprive me of my job, my house, my family, and so on, is a most unpleasant idea and I don't think I want it. You're young, and you can play with these ideas. All the same, I will listen and see what the outcome of this discussion will be"

The students looked at him with that superiority of freedom, with that sense of not being committed to a family, to a group, or to a political or religious party. They had said they were neither Capitalists nor Communists; they were not concerned with political activity at all. They smiled with tolerance and a certain feeling of awkwardness. There is that gap which exists between the older and the younger generations, and they were not going to try to bridge it.

"We are the uncommitted," the student went on, "and therefore we are not hypocrites. Of course we don't know what we want to do, but we know what is not right. We don't want social, racial differences, we're not concerned with all these silly religious beliefs and superstitions, nor do we want political leaders—though there must be a totally different kind of politics which will prevent wars. So we are really concerned, and we want to be involved in the possibilities of man's total transformation. So to put the question again: Firstly, what is this thing that is going to make us change? And secondly—change to what?"

K: Surely, the second question is involved in the first, isn't it? If you already know what you are changing to, is that change at all? If one knows what one will be tomorrow, then "what will be" is already in the present. The future is the present; the known future is the known present. The future is the projection, modified, of what is known now.

"Yes, I see that very clearly. So there is only, then, the question of change, not the verbal definition of what we change to. So we'll limit ourselves to the first question. How do we change? What is the drive, the motive, the force that will make us break down all barriers?"

K: Only complete inaction, only the complete negation of "what is." We do not see the great force that is in negation. If you reject the whole structure of principle and formula, and hence the power derived from it, the authority, that very rejection gives you the force necessary to reject all other structures of thought—and so you have the energy to change! The rejection is that energy.

"Is this what you call 'dying' to the historical accumulation which is the present?"

K: Yes. That very dying is to be born anew. There you have the whole movement of change—the dying to the known.

"Is this rejection a positive, definite act?"

K: When the students revolt it is a positive, definite act, but such action is only very partial and fragmentary. It is not a total rejection. When you ask: "Is it a positive act, this dying, this rejection?"—it is and it isn't. When you positively leave a house and enter into another house, your positive action ceases to be positive action at all because you have abandoned one power structure for another, which you will again have to leave. So this constant repetition, which appears to be a positive action, is really inaction. But if you reject the desire and the search for all inward security, then it is a total negation which is a most positive action. It is this action only which transforms man. If you reject hate and envy, in every form, you are rejecting the whole structure of what man has created in himself and outside himself. It is very simple. One problem is related to every other problem.

"So is this what you call 'seeing the problem'?"

K: This seeing reveals the whole structure and nature of the problem. The "seeing" is not the analyzing of the problem; it is not the revealing of the cause and the effect. It is all there, laid out, as it were, on a map. It is there for you to see, and you can see it only if you have no stand from which to look, and this is our difficulty. We are committed, and inwardly it gives us great pleasure to "belong." When we belong, then it is not possible to see; when we belong, we become irrational, violent, and then we want to end violence by belonging to something else. And so we are caught in a vicious circle. And this is what man has done for millions of years, and he vaguely calls this "evolution." Love is not at the end of time. Either it is now, or it isn't. And hell is when it is not, and the reformation of hell is the decoration of the same hell.

The Role of Fear and Desire

One has been wondering, and you must also have been asking yourself, why we, who have gathered here, who have listened for so many years, why don't we change? What is the root cause of it? Is there one cause? Or are there many causes? We know what the world has become outwardly, more and more fragmented, more and more violent, more insane, one group fighting another group, where we cannot share all the energy of the world for all its people—you know what is happening. And what is our relationship to that, the world and oneself? Are we separate from all that? I question if we are so very radically different from the world about us. With all the competing gurus, the competing religions, the contradictory, opposing ideas and so on, what shall we do together to change ourselves? I am asking this in all seriousness: why we lead our lives as we do, with our petty little ideals, vanities, and all the stupidities that we have accumulated, why is it that we go on in this way?

Is it that we are frightened to change? Is it that we have no desire or intention or urge to find a different way of living? Please ask yourself these questions. I am asking these questions for you, I am not asking for myself. What is the essence of this deterioration of the human mind, and therefore the disintegration in action? Why is there this mind that has become so small, inclusive, not bringing in everything and operating from the whole, but living in a small little courtyard? What is the root of it? Go on, let us talk it over a little bit.

The other day you were asking: Why is it that I have heard you for fifty-two or forty years and I have not changed at all? There have been little changes, modifications, perhaps I am no longer a nationalist, no longer belong to any particular organized group of religious thinking, don't superficially belong to any sect or to any guru—to all that circus that goes on. But deeply one remains more or less the same. Perhaps more refined, the self-centeredness is a little less active, less aggressive, more refined, more yielding, a little more considerate, but the root remains. Have you noticed this? Why? We are talking about the eradication of that root, not the peripheral frills and the peripheral clipping. We are talking about the very root of one's active conscious, or unconscious, egocentricity.

Is it because we need time? Please go into it. Time. Give me time. Man has existed for millions and millions of years; that root has not been uprooted and put aside. Time has not solved it. Right? Please give your mind to this. Evolution, which is the movement of time, has not solved this. We have better bathrooms, better communications, and so on, but the human being is essentially what he was a million years ago. It is a tragic thing if one realizes it. And if one is serious, not just while you are here in this tent, but serious right through your daily life, don't you ever ask: Can this self-centered activity with all its problems ever end? If you asked it seriously, realizing that time and thought—we went into it the other day—are similar, they are the same movement, and thought and time have not solved this problem. And that is the only instrument we have. And we never seem to realize that that instrument, which is the movement of thought, limited as it is, cannot solve the problems. And yet we hold on to that. We hold on to the old instrument.

Thought has created all these problems. That is obvious. The problems of nationality, problems that war creates, problems of religions, all that is the movement of thought which is limited. And that very thought has created this center. Obviously. And yet we don't seem to be able to find a new instrument. We don't find a new instrument but we cannot let go the old instrument, and holding on to it we hope to find the new. You follow? You must let go of something to find the new, right? If you see a path leading up to the top of the mountain and it doesn't lead you up there, you investigate. You don't stick to that path. So one asks: Why is it that human beings are so incredibly stupid? They have wars, they have this fragmentation of nationalities, of religions, all the rest of it, and yet they live in this miserably, unhappy, quarreling, with conflicts, strife—you follow?

Now what will make a human being let go the old instrument and look for the new? You understand? Look for the new. Is it that we are lazy? Is it that we are frightened? Is it, if I let go of this, will you guarantee the other? You understand? Which means one has lived with this limited thought, and one thinks one has found security in that and is afraid to let that go, and yet it is only when there is abandonment of the old that you can find the new. Obviously.

So is it, we are asking, fear? Because you observe the multiplication of gurus all over the world guaranteeing security; "Do this, follow this, practice this, and you will have something at the end of it." That is, a reward. The promise of a reward has a certain fascination and you hope you will find security in that. But when you examine it a little more closely and are not so gullible, do not swallow everything the other fellow says, then you find very clearly that the reward is the reaction from punishment. Because we are trained to the idea of reward and punishment, right? This is obvious. So to escape from punishment, which means pain, grief, and all that, we search for a reward and hope to find in that some kind of security, some kind of peace, some kind of happiness. But when you go into it you don't find it. The gurus and the priests may promise it, but they are just words, right?

So how do we, human beings, go into this question together as to whether it is possible to eradicate totally this poisonous self-interest, self-centered activity? I do not know if you have ever even asked that question. When you do you have already begun to be a little more intelligent. Naturally. So we are going this morning to think this problem over together. Thinking together—not, I tell you and you accept or reject, but together find out if this movement of the ego, the self, can ever end. Are you interested in this? No, don't nod your heads. This is a very serious problem. You may be stimulated while you are in the tent by the speaker—and I hope you are not. But you may be and therefore get rather excited and say, "Yes, I agree with you, we must do this"—and when you leave the tent you forget all about it and carry on in your old ways. So together, you putting aside your particular prejudice, your particular gurus, your particular conclusions, together we are going to investigate this question.

To investigate you must be free. That is obvious, isn't it? You must be free to examine, you must be free from those blocks that impede your examination. The impediments are your prejudices, your experience, your own knowledge, or other people's knowledge, all those act as impediments, and then you cannot possibly have the capacity to examine or think together. At least see this intellectually. The speaker has none of these problems, he has no prejudices, no beliefs either. Finished. And we can only meet together if you are also in that same position.

So let us examine, think over, think together. To think together over the question why human beings throughout the world have remained self-centered. Knowing all the problems it entails, knowing all the confusion, misery, sorrow it involves, they hold on to it, right? Now we are asking: is it desire? You know what desire is? Is desire the root of this self-centered activity? What is desire? You all desire so many things: there is desire for enlightenment, desire for happiness, desire for good looks, desire for what?—a world that will be peaceful?—desire to fulfill and avoid frustration? Desire by which all human beings are driven. Do you follow this? We are asking, is that one of the root causes of this self-centered existence with all its confusion and misery?

And religions throughout the world have said you must suppress desire. You must become a monk in the service of God, and to attain that supreme thing you must have no desire. This has been the constant repetition of all the so-called religious people in the world. And without understanding the structure and nature of desire, they have had this ideal that to serve the highest principle, Brahman in India, God or Christ in the Christian world, or other forms of religious sectarian nonsense, you suppress, control, dominate desire.

Now together we are going to look into what is desire. Please listen carefully. When you analyze what is desire, you are using thought as a means of analysis. That is, going into the past. You are following this? And so you are using the old instrument, which is limited thought, and looking into the past, step by step, which is the whole psychoanalytical process. But to examine desire you must see the actuality of it, not move it back. Please come with me a little bit. You must be very clear on this point. The psychoanalytical, introspective self-examination process is going backwards, and thereby hoping to find the cause. To do that you employ thought, right? And thought is limited, the old instrument, you are using the old instrument to find the root of desire.

Now we are saying something entirely different. Please give a little attention to it. We are saying analysis by oneself, or by the professional, doesn't lead anywhere, unless you are slightly neurotic and all the rest of it, then it may be a little helpful. Perhaps we are all slightly neurotic! We are saying: observe the nature of desire. Don't analyze, just observe. You understand the difference? Is this clear? I am going to show it to you. Must everything be explained, which is too bad! You don't jump to it and say, "Yes, I have got it." All that you say is, "Explain, and I will get it, explain the whole movement of desire, employ the correct words, describe it precisely and I'll get it." What you get is the clarity of explanation, clarity of words, but that doesn't give you the total observation of the movement of desire.

So can you stop analyzing but just observe? Have you got it? Are we meeting each other? One can describe the beauty of the mountain, the white snow, the blue sky, the marvelous dignity and the glory of it, the valleys, the rivers, the streams, the flowers, and most of us are satisfied with the explanations. We don't say, "I'll go, get up and climb and find out."

We are going into this question of desire very carefully, not the movement of tracing it back and thereby hoping to find the nature of desire. But actively together to look at it. What is desire? Look at it yourself. Together we are doing it. You desire a dress, which you see in the window, and there is the response. You like the color, the shape, the fashion, and desire says, "Let me go and buy it." So what has taken place actually at that moment? Which is not analysis, but actually observing the reaction to the seeing of that dress in the window, and the response to that. Don't go to sleep, please.

You see that dress, you like the color, you like the fashion—what has taken place there? You observe, there is the sensation, right? There is contact, you touch it, then desire arises through the image which thought has built of you putting on that dress. Do you understand this? Seeing, sensation, contact, then thought imagining that dress on you and then desire. You follow this? Not follow me, the fact of it. I have only given an explanation, the words, but we are talking of the actual response; the seeing, contact, sensation, thought imagining that dress on you, and desire is born. Have you got this? No, it is not yours, not mine.

Now wait, follow this carefully. The moment thought creates the image, from that image desire is born, right? Please understand this. I am bored with explanations! I will stick to that dress, or the shirt. There is perception of that in the window, the seeing, the visual optic response, then going inside, touching the material, then thought says, "How nice it would be if I had it." And imagines that you are wearing it. That is the moment of desire. Do you see this, actually, not see my explanation and through that explanation you see? Is that clear, that you yourself observe the happening?

Now the question is—please go into it carefully—why does thought create the image of you having that shirt, that dress, and then pursuing it? Watch it. Think it out. Go into it. Exercise your brains. One sees a blue shirt. Then you see it, go and touch it, feel the material, then thought comes and says, "How nice." Then the question is: Can thought abstain from creating the image? You understand my question? I will explain, take time, go into it.

We are examining the whole movement of desire because we are asking: Is desire the very root of this self-centered, egotistic existence? And from that we are asking: What is desire? And the speaker is totally opposed—totally opposed—to suppression because that doesn't solve the problem. He says, Don't run away from it into a monastery, into taking vows, and all those kinds of things—that is merely avoidance. What we are saying is: Examine it, look at it, not analytically, but as it is taking place, observe it. The observation shows the optic response to the blue dress, blue shirt, the contact by going into the shop, touching the material, then thought creates the image, and desire is born. It is only when thought creates the image that desire comes into being. Otherwise it does not. Are you together in this?

So desire comes into being and flowers the moment that thought creates the image. You have had a pleasant experience, sexual or whatever. And it has created an image, a picture, and you pursue it. One is a form of pleasure, the other is the movement of contradictory desires—right? You desire that dress—or desire great success, and so on. Now can you observe this fact, that the moment when thought creates the image, desire is born? Are you aware of this? Do you see it as it happens? How thought creates through its imagination the desire to pursue to the very end? Do you now, sitting there, actually observe this fact for yourself? Obviously. It is very simple. Right?

The question arises then: Can thought not create the image? That is the whole point. Am I making this terribly difficult? We have come to the point when you yourself observe the springing up of desire, right? Perception, seeing, contact, sensation. Up to then there is no desire. It is just reaction. But the moment thought creates the image the whole cycle begins. Do you see this? If you see it clearly, then the question arises: Why does thought always create this image? Why? You see a shirt, red, blue, white, whatever it is, there is instantly like and dislike, which means thought brings in its previous experiences, and so on.

So can you observe the blue shirt, dress in the window, and realize the nature of thought, and see that the moment that thought comes in, the problem begins? Not only the blue shirt or dress or your sexual experiences, but the image that you have of a position, a status, a function—the pictures, the thinking over. So desire is that. And can you observe without the inflaming desire coming into being? Go into it, you will see it. You can do it. That is the new instrument, which is to observe.

Then there is desire for security—they are the same thing, security in terms of a big house, little house, bank account, which may be necessary, and also security that desire has created about oneself, the image that you have about yourself, and the fulfillment of that image in action. In that is involved many kinds of frustration, and in spite of the frustrations, in spite of conflicts, misery, desire goes on pursuing, because thought is always creating the image where there is sensation. I wonder if you see this?

So the next question we are asking is: Is desire responsible for fear? We have sought security through desire and the fulfillment of that desire, psychologically, in God—I don't want to go on and on about this!—and unconsciously, deeply one may be aware that the things in which you have invested, desire has invested, have no value at all. And having no value, you are frightened. Are you following this, because again, we are not analyzing fear. That is a stupid old game. We are observing the actual fact of fear. And as it arises, to observe, ask: What is the root of it? Not discover this by analysis, but in the very observation of it you discover the root. Do you get it? You seem rather doubtful. I am going to go into this.

The human being has accepted and lived with fear. Outwardly with the fear of violence, fear of getting hurt physically, and so on. And inwardly, psychologically, with the fear of not conforming to a pattern, fear of public opinion, of not achieving, not fulfillling, and so on. We are asking, can you observe that fact—without the analytical mind operating on the fact—and observe the whole movement of fear, as it exists?

Are you getting tired? Ten minutes more. Bear up with it! Because you see it is possible to be absolutely free of fear psychologically. Don't accept my word for it, it is your life, not mine, it is yours, you have to find this out.

So you have to ask: What is fear? Has it roots in desire? Go into it slowly, don't say no. Go into it. Desire being what we have said: thought creating the image and then pursuing that image which it might fulfill and might not. You follow? If it fulfills there is no fear, or at least there are other calamities involved in it. But when there is no fulfillment there is frustration and the fear of not being able to fulfill—this whole complex sexual fulfillment, which apparently the world is now just discovering and making a lot of noise about—promiscuity and all the rest of it. So we are asking: Is fear the product of desire? Desire being the image formation and the fulfillment of that image in action. Or is fear—please follow this carefully—part of time? You understand? Is fear the movement of time? So are desire and time responsible for fear? Oh, my Lord! I will explain, I will explain. Go slowly.

Desire is the movement of thought with its imagery. That is, the movement of thought creating the image, and the movement of that image, which is time, right? Not chronological time, but psychological time. And we are asking: Is time also responsible for fear? The time of desire—ah, I am getting it. The time which desire creates, and thought which has created the desire, and thought being also time, so thought and desire are responsible for fear. You see that? Say I am afraid of what you might do to me. I am afraid you might hurt me psychologically. I am afraid that dog will bite me. But at the moment of biting, time has come to an end. It is only that the dog might bite me. I have created the image, thought has created the image of that dog biting, which is time, in the future. You are following all this? So desire has its future and time is naturally future, the past, present, and future.

So the question is: Can thought realize its own movement creating fear? You understand? Thought realizing its own nature. When it realizes its own nature, as the active principle in fear, what takes place? There is only then what is actually happening. I wonder if you see that? Do please, come. Because it would be worthwhile if we could think together about this matter. Then you will leave the tent having understood the movement of fear, and realizing the nature of desire, and the nature of limited thought creating time, which is fear. Do you realize it? Or have you merely accepted the words? If you realize it, the thing is over. There are no gurus, no gods, all that nonsense.

Q: My thought does not stop.

K: No, it is not a question of thought stopping. We will discuss that a little later when we talk about meditation, if you are interested. But that is not the point. I am saying: Does thought itself realize what it is doing? That it has created the desire, and the fulfillment of that desire is time. And in that is involved fear. And also thought has created what might happen. There has been pain; I hope there won't be pain again, which is in the future. So thought has created the future, right? And the future is the very nature of fear. I wonder if you get it?

Look, if I die instantly there is no fear. If I have an immediate heart attack—*phut*, gone—there is no fear. But my heart is weak, I might die, which is the future. The future is the movement of fear. Get it? See the truth of it, not your conclusion. Not your saying, "Yes, I see it," but see the truth of it.

Then that very truth operates. You don't have to do a thing. If you see that truth, and that truth being the fact, then thought says, "All right, I have finished." Thought cannot operate on a fact. It can operate on something that is non-fact. So after having listened to this verbiage, have you realized the nature of fear? See the truth of it. If you really see the truth of it, fear has gone. It is not that you control thought. You are the thought. You understand? It is one of our peculiar conditionings that you are different from thought, and therefore you say, "I will control thought." But when you realize that thought itself is the "me," and that thought has created this future, which is fear, and see the truth of it—not intellectually, you can't see the truth intellectually, you can see intellectually a clear, verbal explanation, but that is not the truth—the truth is the fact that the future, the whole movement of the future, is giving birth to fear.

Now you have listened to this, perhaps in different ways, and to different explanations on different occasions, and you are gathered here again, and you have listened this morning to a very clear explanation, which is not analysis, and are you free of fear? That is the test. If you are still carrying on, and say, "I am afraid of . . ."—you know, all the rest of that business, then you haven't really listened.

Pressure Does Not Change Us

Before we begin to bombard each other with a lot of questions and arguments, I wonder if you have read in the newspaper—I don't generally read newspapers, I look at the headlines—that the world every year is spending four hundred billion dollars on armaments. That is four hundred thousand million dollars. I don't know what that sum means, but that is what is being spent on trying to kill each other. I wonder, after reading such a statement, what will make human beings change? Yesterday, that gentleman on my left put a question: he said I have listened to you for so many years, listened to your talks, listened to your tapes and so on, and I am exactly where I started when I began. I think it would be important if we could go into that question rather seriously. Perhaps most of us are in that position—perhaps.

What will make a human being change very deeply? This has been a great problem for people concerned with the transformation of man. What makes us change? If you put that question to yourself seriously, and ask it with all the depth of your being, what will make you change? Will an external event bring about a crisis in your life, and that force you to do some radical thinking, and change? A death in the family, an incident or an event, or a happening that is devastating, psychologically as well as physically—will that bring about deep change? Must you go through great pain, great sorrow, great agony, brought about by external events, that forces you, forces a human being, to alter his course, his drive, his direction, his selfishness, his limited, brutal thinking? We have had several wars, and most of us perhaps have lived through two wars, devastating wars, millions have been killed. Think of the misery, the confusion, and enormous sorrow of those people who have had great losses, not only material losses but also their sons destroyed. And outer events, however great they are, don't apparently seem to bring about a freedom so that we can say, "This cannot happen again."

So I am asking you—this has been a question that we have considered many, many times—will external events change human beings? That is one problem. Such events have apparently not changed man—change in the sense of a real deep transformation of this selfish drive, identified with groups, with nations, with beliefs, dogmas, religion, and all the rest of it. And apparently—please follow this—apparently some outward event, like the death of one's husband, wife, children, does through great pain and sorrow bring a certain change in oneself. I do not know if you have noticed it. Does that mean we must depend on external events—death, war, somebody leaving you, and so on—external devastating events, will that change you? Which means that you must depend on outward things, which will then put you through great agony and suffering and out of that you emerge, bringing about perhaps a deep mutation.

It seems to us that that is the most appalling thing, even to say, that we must go through suffering to bring about change. That is inconceivable, but yet apparently that is what happens. It is like a man who drives a car rather carelessly, kills others and survives, and afterward he says, "I am going to be awfully careful how I drive." He is intelligent after the event. Is it possible to be intelligent before the event? By "intelligence" meaning not to become more clever in this instinctual survival of selfishness, of that drive of desire, and so on, but intelligence that is born of the perception that outward events do not fundamentally change man, but that change must come totally inwardly, without any pressure, without any incident or event. To perceive that is part of intelligence. To perceive the truth that if I depend on outward pressure, outward events which put me through a great deal of sorrow and anxiety, I will either become cynical and bitter or escape into some form of entertainment. So in that there is no deep change. To see that is part of intelligence. The materialists, the Communists, the totalitarian people say change the outward events, then human beings change. But that has been tried through millennia, and apparently they have not changed.

Also, there is this statement made by several gurus and teachers in the East, and perhaps in the West, that if you surrender yourself, then all your problems are solved. You again surrender to something outside, or surrender to something that you have created. Please, are we understanding each other? This is very important after the question of that gentleman yesterday. He said, "I have listened to you for so many years and I have not changed. I am where I started out." You know to hear such a statement, you cry inwardly. I wonder how many of you cried inwardly. And what will change him, or you, or another? Is it, as we said, an external, devastating event, which brings about sorrow? And if the sorrow is deep, it shatters everything that you have had, and then perhaps you say, "I can't live this way anymore"—so you are again depending on an external event? And external events can be vast, like wars, earthquakes, and so on. Realizing that these religious—can I use the word "exploiters"?—these religious exploiters—with your consent I am using that word—say, Give yourself over, surrender. You understand the implications of it? Surrender of course to the guru, to the man who says, "Surrender," but inwardly do you eliminate this drive, this self-centeredness? Again it is the same phenomenon, which is pressure, and now you are exerting inward pressure to submit to somebody else. Have you understood this? Can we go on from there?

Now do you listen to all this—that outward pressure is not going to change you and inward giving yourself over to a presence, a reality, to God, to this or to that, is still desire driving you to forget yourself, but the self is still there, only covered up. So do you listen to these statements? Or it doesn't mean a thing? So perhaps the root of the matter lies there: intellectually, verbally you see reasonably, logically, the very clear statements we have made just now, unless you want to change the words, but the essential point is the outward pressure through sorrow, and the inward drive to escape from yourself, which again is another form of pressure. Do you listen to this, so that you see the truth: that whether it is pressure from outside or from inside there is no change? To see that, to hear that, and see that fact, is intelligence. So are you, forgive me for asking this question, are you, who have listened to this, clearly expounded, logically, sanely, do you see the actuality of it, the truth of it and therefore there is intelligence? Therefore that intelligence is the denial of the outer or the inner, and therefore moving from where you are.

Now have you taken it in, seriously gone into it as we did just now, and seen that outward or inward pressure in different forms, in different ways, will not bring about a radical mutation? To hear that and see it is intelligence. Do you see it? Do you have that intelligence? Therefore that intelligence acts before the event, so that one has not to go through sorrow. If you discover that, it is something—you follow—it is a divine gift. Sorry to use the word "divine." It is a great, enormous gift because when one realizes that a catastrophic, devastating event that brings sorrow, or any outward or inner pressure will not change one, when one sees that, the truth of it, before the event or pressure takes place, then that intelligence is operating wherever it is, whether in your daily life, whether it is in an office, it is operating all the time.

The Destructiveness of Attachment

QUESTIONER: We are medical students in college, why is it we never notice things in the way you do? Why are we not serious enough to change ourselves?

KRISHNAMURTI: Does this apply only to medical students? Or does it apply to most of us? We never notice the morning clouds, the parrots, and their wayward flight. We never notice the dog on the wayside or the goats that lie in the middle of the road. We never notice the beauty of a tree. And why is it, the questioner says, that we do not change? What is the root of all this? In a civilization like India's, which has probably existed for three to four thousand years, a culture that has almost disappeared, which has now become extraordinarily mundane, worldly, money-minded, corrupt, and all the rest of it, why it is that we don't change? Ask yourself, if you are serious enough, why is it I don't change, what is it that prevents us? Is it financial security, physical stability, which we are seeking? That's one point. Is it that we are intellectually unable to discern, to distinguish, to understand, to be critical, to sustain a skeptical outlook on life? Is it that emotionally we are starved? We are very sensuous people, wanting sex and pleasure, and therefore demanding money, position, power, ambition, and all the rest of it—is this what is preventing us? Because we are, all of us, from childhood, from the moment the baby is born it seeks security—physical and psychological security. It wants to be safe with the mother; if anyone dislikes the mother the baby feels it. This has been tested out in the West, not here.

The question is why, realizing all this, do we not change? Or we never realize this fact? We just carry on in the good old tradition. And our brains have become so accustomed to this pattern of living that they refuse to change, because it is very comfortable to live in a pattern. Is that the reason why we don't change? Is it that we do not have enough physical and psychological energy? We have plenty of energy. You go to the office every day for the rest of your life; that indicates a great deal of energy. And there is the energy that we waste through quarrels, cruelty, and indifference. We have got plenty of energy. And again, why don't we change, we know all this? Some of you have perhaps heard the speaker for the last thirty, forty, fifty years and there is very little change. Why? Answer it yourselves. Why is it that we have become so dull? Is it the tradition, your religion, your sacred books? I am asking you, please investigate with me. Are all these the reasons why we don't change?

It is natural and healthy to want security; you need food, clothes, and shelter, everyone does, that is natural. And is there security psychologically, which we also want? We want security in our relationship, however intimate or not, we want to be quite sure my wife, my husband, remains with me. We are so terribly attached. If one could understand the nature of attachment with all its consequences, and see the very danger of such attachment, which denies love, if one really saw that and dropped it immediately, then perhaps some change can take place. But we don't. You hear this, that attachment in any form to anything is very, very corrupting, destructive. When you are attached to somebody or to a principle, an ideal, a belief, you are not only separating yourself from another but from that attachment to a belief, a person, an ideal, there is fear, jealousy, anxiety, a sense of possessive pleasure, and therefore always a state of inward uncertainty. One knows the consequences of attachment.

Now, would you change that immediately, or just listen, fold your hands most respectfully, and turn up the next day while we talk about attachment? You understand my question? Why are we so sluggish? You ask yourself.

One realizes that basically, deeply, one doesn't want to change, and therefore there are various forms of escape. There are not only drugs, chemical drugs one takes in order to escape from one's narrow, ugly, sloppy life, one takes them to have more experience and have a different vision, through alcohol, LSD, marijuana, all those things that are going on in this world. Why is our mind so dull that we don't see danger and change immediately? Do please go into it. This is real sorrow. This incapacity to bring about a change in ourselves and therefore in society, in our relationship, this incapacity makes one not only time-bound, but we don't flower, we don't grow, we don't move. So what is one to do? Do you want more shocks, more pain, more suffering to make one change?

So there are those people who say, As human beings will not change, therefore create a society that will control the human being—the Communist world, the totalitarian world, the socialist world. The more uncertain we are, as is now the case in the world, the more insecure, we turn to tradition, we turn to gurus, or join some political party. All this is going on, if you have realized it. So at the end of all this, why don't we change? You understand? Is it utter unwillingness, utter stupidity?

When you observe all this right through the world, it is a very sad affair. There is marvelous technology, which is growing at such immense speed, and man cannot keep up with it psychologically, and so he is going to destroy human beings. I don't know if you are aware of all this. So what are you going to do? Carry on as before? Probably you will.

"I should Be Doing Something Else"

QUESTIONER: I feel that my daily life is unimportant, that I should be doing something else.

KRISHNAMURTI: When you are eating, eat. When you are going for a walk, walk. Don't say, "I must be doing something else." When you are reading give your attention completely to that, whether it is a detective novel, a magazine, the Bible, or what you will. Complete attention is complete action, and therefore there is no "I must be doing something else." It is only when we are inattentive that we have the feeling of "By Jove, I must do something better." If we give complete attention when we are eating, that is action. What is important is not what we are doing but whether we can give total attention. I mean by that word not something we learn through concentration in a school or in business, but to attend, with our bodies, our nerves, our eyes, our ears, our minds, our hearts—completely. If we do that there is a tremendous crisis in our lives. Then something demands our whole energy, vitality, attention. Life demands that attention every minute, but we are so trained to inattention that we are always trying to escape from attention to inattention. We say, "How am I to attend? I am lazy." Be lazy, but be totally attentive to the laziness. Be totally attentive to inattention. Know that you are completely inattentive. Then when you know that you are totally attentive to inattention, you are attentive.

How Are You Listening?

Before we begin our dialogue, I think we ought to clear up some points. We seem to be blocking ourselves. Some say that what you are talking about is not possible. It can never be applied in daily life. "I have listened to you for twenty, thirty, forty, fifty years and nothing has happened, I am just the same as before." That is a block that prevents the person who says this from investigating himself. He has blocked himself by saying, "It is not possible." That is obvious.

And also there are those who say, "I understand partially, but I want to understand the whole before I can do something about it." Again, that is a block. Again, that prevents your own investigation of yourself, you are blocking yourself.

And there are those who say, "What you are saying is totally impractical, why don't you stop talking and go away?" Such people, and I have heard this very often, not only prevent their own investigation of themselves, but also because one person can't do it he condemns the rest of the world—"If I can't do it, you can't do it." And so this goes on.

Let me talk a little, and then we will have a dialogue. If we could this morning realize, if I may point out, that we are not a thousand or two thousand people in the tent, but we are two people talking to each other. You and the speaker are talking together. When we two talk together it includes all the others, it is bound to. And I would like to point out, if I may again, please don't hinder yourself by blocking yourself, by saying, "I can't do this, it is impossible. You are a biological freak, and this is not applicable to ordinary people. You have to have special genes to understand all this." One finds innumerable excuses; one finds every form of avoidance of looking into one's own hindrances, observing them closely, understanding them, and trying to put them aside. If we could do that, then perhaps we could have better communication with each other.

And also I would like to point out that I think we don't listen, we don't really try to find out what the other person is trying to say. And listening requires a certain attention, care, affection. If I want to understand what you are saying, I must listen to you, not block myself all the way, all the time. I must care for what you are saying, I must have respect, I must have affection, love, otherwise we can't communicate certain things which are really very, very serious and require a great deal of inquiry. So may I suggest that we listen with affection, with care? We want to assert our own points of view, we want to exercise our own opinions and dominate others by our judgments, our conclusions, by our asserting that we have listened to you for so long, and asking why we haven't changed. All that indicates, it seems to me, and I may be wrong, that there is no real love. I am not blaming anybody, I am just stating this. Don't get angry, don't ride a high horse!

And I think we should go very deeply into why we don't listen. Or we say, "Yes, I have listened, I have listened to you for twenty years, it is all over. I am not going to listen to you any more." You don't say that to a child, do you, whom you love? He wants to tell you something, he may tell it to you ten times, he has already told you, but the next time he says something, you listen. You don't brush him aside, you are not impatient, you love that child. And I think in all these discussions and dialogues and talks, we are missing that essential perfume. I don't think we know what it is to listen with love, which doesn't mean that we shouldn't be critical, which doesn't mean that we should accept everything that is said. Neither does it mean that we agree or disagree. You listen, listen with care, with affection, with a sense of communication with each other. And for that one must have love. And probably that is what is missing. We are all too terribly intellectual, or too romantic, or too sentimental. All that denies love.

So perhaps, if we could this morning have a dialogue on whatever subject you want, bearing in mind that without this quality of affection, care, love, and compassion, we merely play with words, remain superficial, antagonistic, assertive, dogmatic, and so on. It remains merely verbal; it has no depth, no quality, no perfume. So bearing that in mind, what subject would you like to talk about?

Appendix

Since Krishnamurti's death, schools that seek to apply his approach to education have continued in India, the United States, and England.

The Brockwood Park School in England is residential, international, and coeducational and provides secondary and higher education for fifteen- to twenty-four-year-olds.

The Krishnamurti Study Centre accommodates adult guests who wish to study Krishnamurti's works in quiet surroundings, whether by the day, on weekends, or for a week or so.

The Krishnamurti Foundation Trust maintains the Krishnamurti archives and distributes books, and audio and video recordings.

The following is the address for all three organizations:

Brockwood Park School
Bramdean
Hampshire, SO24 0LQ
England

Additional contact information for these three organizations is as follows:

Brockwood Park School
Phone: 44 1962 771 744
Fax: 44 1962 771 875

E-mail: admin@brockwood.org.uk
www.brockwood.org.uk

The Krishnamurti Study Centre
Phone: 44 1962 771 748
E-mail: kCentre@brockwood.org.uk
www.brockwood.org.uk

The Krishnamurti Foundation Trust
Phone: 44 1962 771 525
Fax: 44 1962 771 159
E-mail: info@brockwood.org.uk
www.kfoundation.org

For information about the Krishnamurti Foundation of America, the Oak Grove School, and the Retreat Center, please contact:

The Krishnamurti Foundation of America
P.O. Box 1560
Ojai, CA 93024-1560
U.S.A.
E-mail: kfa@kfa.org
www.kfa.org

Source Notes

Are You Not Saying What the Buddha Said?

A conversation at Brockwood Park on 22 June 1978. Reprinted by
permission of HarperCollins Publishers, London, from *Questioning Krishnamurti* © 1978 Krishnamurti Foundation Trust,
Ltd.

Is There a State of Mind without the Self?

First conversation at Brockwood Park on 23 June 1978, © 1978
Krishnamurti Foundation Trust, Ltd.

Free Will, Action, Love, and Identification and the Self

Second conversation at Brockwood Park on 23 June 1978, © 1978
Krishnamurti Foundation Trust, Ltd.

What Is Truth?

First conversation at Brockwood Park on 28 June 1979. Reprinted
by permission of HarperCollins Publishers, London, from *On
Truth* © 1995 Krishnamurti Foundation Trust, Ltd and Krishnamurti Foundation of America.

Life after Death

Second conversation at Brockwood Park on 28 June 1979, © 1979
Krishnamurti Foundation Trust, Ltd.

Why Don't We Change?

"Questioner: After having listened eagerly . . . seeking to achieve an end." From the talk at Bombay on 4 March 1956.

"The priests throughout the world . . . without the least effort." From the tape of the talk at Saanen on 15 July 1976.

"Can we as human beings . . . That is the whole point." From the tape of the talk at Brockwood Park on 25 August 1979.

"It seems to me . . . That is the real question." From the talk at Varanasi on 22 November 1965 in *The Collected Works of J. Krishnamurti* © 1991 Krishnamurti Foundation of America.

"*There were four or five people* . . . of the same hell." From the first of *Five Conversations* © 1968 Krishnamurti Foundation Trust, Ltd.

"One has been wondering . . . you haven't really listened." From the talk at Saanen on 17 July 1979.

"Before we begin to bombard . . . operating all the time." From the talk at Saanen on 27 July 1978.

"Questioner: We are medical students . . . probably you will." From the Question and Answer meeting at Madras on 7 October 1981.

"Questioner: I feel that my daily life is . . . you are attentive." From the talk at Saanen on 28 July 1966 in *The Collected Works of J. Krishnamurti* © 1991 Krishnamurti Foundation of America.

"Before we begin . . . like to talk about?" From the talk at Saanen on 26 July 1979.

Books by J. Krishnamurti

Can Humanity Change?: J. Krishnamurti in Dialogue with Buddhists

Many have considered Buddhism to be the religion closest in spirit to J. Krishnamurti's spiritual teaching—even though the great teacher was famous for urging students to seek truth outside organized religion. This record of a historic encounter between Krishnamurti and a group of Buddhist scholars provides a unique opportunity to see what the great teacher had to say himself about Buddhist teachings.

Facing a World in Crisis: What Life Teaches Us in Challenging Times

Facing a World in Crisis presents a selection of talks that Krishnamurti gave on how to live and respond to troubling and uncertain times. His message of personal responsibility and the importance of connecting with the broader world is presented in a nonsectarian and nonpolitical way. Direct and ultimately life-affirming, this book will resonate with readers looking for a new way to understand and find hope in challenging times.

Freedom, Love, and Action

In *Freedom, Love, and Action*, Krishnamurti points to a state of total awareness beyond mental processes. With his characteristic engaging, candid approach, Krishnamurti discusses such topics as the importance of setting the mind free from its own conditioning; the possibility of finding enlightenment in everyday activities; the inseparability of freedom, love, and action; and why it is best to love without attachment.

Inward Revolution: Bringing about Radical Change in the World

Here, J. Krishnamurti inquires with the reader into how remembering and dwelling on past events, both pleasurable and painful, give us a false sense of continuity, causing us to suffer. His instruction is to be attentive and clear in our perceptions and to meet the challenges of life directly in each new moment.

Meditations

This classic collection of brief excerpts from Krishnamurti's books and talks presents the essence of his teaching on meditation—a state of attention, beyond thought, that brings total freedom from authority and ambition, fears and separateness.

Talks with American Students

In 1968—a time when young Americans were intensely questioning the values of their society—Krishnamurti gave a series of talks to college students in the United States and Puerto Rico, exploring the true meaning of freedom and rebellion. Collected in this book, these lectures are perhaps even more compelling today, when both adults and young people are searching for the key to genuine change in our world.

This Light in Oneself: True Meditation

These selections present the core of Krishnamurti's teaching on meditation, taken from discussions with small groups, as well as from public talks to large audiences. His main theme is the essential need to look inward, to know ourselves, in order really to understand our own—and the world's—conflicts. He offers timeless insights into the source of true freedom and wisdom.

To Be Human

This book presents Krishnamurti's radical vision of life in a new way. At the heart of this extraordinary collection are passages from the great teacher's talks that amplify and clarify the nature of truth and those obstacles that often prevent us from seeing it. Besides presenting the core of Krishnamurti's message, the book alerts the reader to his innovative use of language, the ways in which he would use "old words with new interpretations," then gives practical examples, showing that we can clarify our understanding of life itself—and act on this new understanding.